THE
NEW GUIDE
TO HERBS

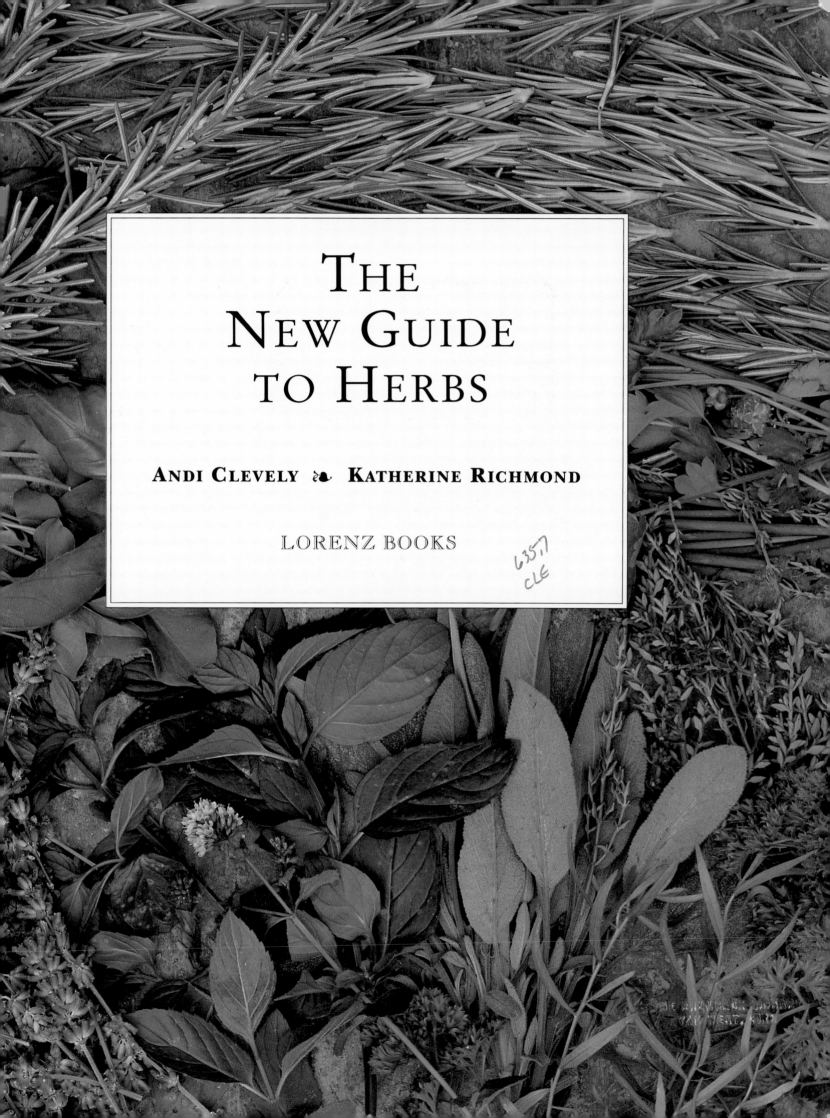

THE
NEW GUIDE
TO HERBS

ANDI CLEVELY ❧ **KATHERINE RICHMOND**

LORENZ BOOKS

Paperback edition first published in 1998 by Lorenz Books
27 West 20th Street, New York, NY 10011

LORENZ BOOKS are available for bulk purchase for sales promotion
and for premium use. For details, write or call the sales director,
Lorenz Books, 27 West 20th Street, New York, NY 10011;
(800) 354-9657

ISBN 1-85967-736-3

Publisher: Joanna Lorenz
Senior Editor: Penelope Cream
Photographer: John Freeman
Consultant: Anthony Gardiner

Printed and bound in Singapore

1 3 5 7 9 10 8 6 4 2

ACKNOWLEDGMENTS
The publishers and authors would like to extend special thanks to
Anthony Gardiner for his unfailing enthusiasm and expert advice;
to Warren and Jenny Prestwich at R & G Stevens, Lucas Green Nurseries,
for their generosity and warm hospitality; to Simon and Judith Hopkinson
and their staff at Hollington Nurseries and Rosemary Titterington at
Iden Croft Herbs for all their help and advice.

CONTENTS

Introduction

Juniperus lycia

The history of herbs is as long as the story of mankind, for people have used these plants since earliest times. Wars have been fought and lands conquered for the sake of plants, and even today we continue to depend on exotic species for many of our newest medicines and chemicals.

Today herbs are so pervasive that we take them for granted and barely give them a thought except when cooking or gardening – in contrast to the past when people had a more intimate relationship with the plants around them.

In medieval Europe, country people had always gathered wild harvests of useful plants, but it was in the monastic herb gardens that plants of known virtue were transplanted and organized in beds and borders, and their usefulness studied. This was then catalogued in such early works as the tenth-century book of 'simples' (herbal medicines) sent to Britain by the Patriarch of Jerusalem. and the major treatise on herbs written by a thirteenth-century Franciscan monk, Bartholomaeus Anglicus. Berries, seeds and barks from distant parts of the world were dried and imported as spices to increase the range of flavors and fragrances available to the few who could afford them.

Values change as settled societies become wealthy and less involved in the daily struggle for survival. Before

Left: *An elegantly spiraling clipped yew, flanked by the leafy stems of angelica.*

long herbs were being cultivated in Europe, not just for their availability when needed but also to be enjoyed as amenity plants. This growing appreciation of what is now termed their 'garden merits' seemed to coincide with a gradual decline in their practical use.

In the nineteenth century, prepared medicines, dyes and cosmetics had become widely available, and better methods of food preservation and distribution meant there was no need to use strong herbs and spices to disguise the flavor of rank meat and stale fish. Old herbal wisdom became suspect as primitive and unreliable, so that today in Western societies, herbalism has become synonymous with cranky superstition.

Below: *Illuminations of herbs and flowers were commonly used to decorate medieval Books of Hours.*

NATURAL SWEETENERS

Plants add an almost infinite variety of flavors to food, but only a few contribute obvious sweetness, even though the common names of many herbs include the description 'sweet'. For commercial production sugar cane is an important crop in the tropics, while sugar beet is grown in temperate regions. Tree saps can be evaporated to a syrup for use as sweeteners, notably the sugar maple (Acer saccharatum) of North America, although walnut trees were recommended during the Second World War in Britain as a source of syrup. The best herb for this purpose is European sweet cicely, Myrrhis odorata, *whose leaves can be substituted for some of the sugar needed in acid fruit recipes. In recent years* Lippia dulcis, *a relative of lemon verbena, was identified as the plant the Aztecs called 'sweet herb' and has been found to contain hernandulcin, a substance that is a thousand times sweeter than sucrose.*

Happily, changing fashion is restoring herbs to their former importance. Alternative medicine has rediscovered some of the skills of phytotherapy (the use of medicinal plants), and the ancient pedigree of healing herbs. Concern for the precarious status of many wild species, especially those that grow exclusively in threatened tropical rainforests, has highlighted the unique properties that might be lost with their extinction. An interest in international cuisines has made us familiar with the flavors of oriental lemon grass, leaf coriander from the eastern Mediterranean, and South American

Left: *An intricate herbal border in the fifteenth-century* Siege of Tripoli *by Guillelmus of Tyre.*

maté, the restorative tea brewed from the leaves of a holly, *Ilex paraguayensis.*

Histories of herbs and herb gardens used to be written from a European viewpoint, ignoring the important fact that global human dependence on plants is

Far Left: An example of the popular Victorian art of arranging pressed herbs and flowers.

Left: Nicholas Culpeper, the great seventeenth-century herbalist, who produced the Theatrum Botanicum in 1640.

Below: Heartsease and wild strawberry are among the decorative motifs adorning this Book of Hours by Simon Marmion, c. 1480.

characteristic of all societies in tune with their surroundings, yet Kuna Indians in Panama reserve parts of their forests as sanctuaries in which their healers can gather the medicinal herbs so important to their way of life; the Antasaka and other coastal tribes of Madagascar exploit forest plants for all their clothing, medicines, food and building materials; fishermen on the island of Socotra throw wood chips from the Adenium tree into pools to sedate fish for an easy catch; Arab horsemen treat their mounts with a whole pharmacopoeia of herbs developed by medieval Arabian physicians; and European Romanies still gather wild garlic and wayside herbs as they have done since their migrations began long ago.

Most modern gardeners need to relearn this instinctive affinity with herbs, but growing them in the garden will inevitably lead to an understanding of their qualities. None of us can grow them all, for the choice is vast and increasing as new species and their properties are discovered.

Growing Herbs

Herbs as Garden Plants

There are many definitions of a herb, none altogether satisfactory. To the botanist it is a plant that dies down to ground level at the end of the growing season; medicinally the word refers to any plant that can assist in the prevention or treatment of illness; while in the kitchen it means a part of a plant that is used in the preparation of food.

Arctium lappa

Paradoxically many gardeners grow only a limited choice of herbs for use, planting others according to their ornamental merits. An essential collection might contain parsley, sage, thyme and mint, with rosemary, lavender or marjoram as optional extras.

How far to explore the treasury of herbs depends on your available space, and on the type of climate and terrain enjoyed by your garden. Plants of tropical origin need warm walls or greenhouse protection in temperate regions, while Mediterranean herbs and shrubs with grey or white leaves prefer dry, sunny places similar to their natural habitats. There are herbs for moist dappled shade, parched banks or the boggy margins of pools, for rock gardens, window boxes and patio pots, climbers to train on arches and trellises, and prostrate leafy mats for embellishing the edges of paths and tops of walls.

Many herbs have varieties and cultivars with colored and variegated foliage, and these can be planted to create a satisfying tapestry of contrasting shades. They are usually a little less vigorous than the normal types from which they were bred. The plainer forms might not rival modern hybrid

EARLY HERBALS

*The earliest books about herbs are a fascinating subject for collection and study. Apart from their obvious curiosity value, they are evidence of the beliefs and understandings of particular eras, and chart changing attitudes to plants, the ways in which they act, and their importance in diets, medicine and daily household life, as well as contemporary issues of astrology, alchemy and divination. The earliest scientific works were Theophrastus' *Enquiry into Plants and *Growth of Plants *(c. 300 BC). Seminal texts of the Middle Ages were Avicenna's *Canon Medicinae *(c. 1020) and the Anglo-Saxon Leech Book of Bald *(c. 950).*

Left: *Even a small herb garden can supply a wide range of aromatic, edible and medicinal material for everyday use.*

Right: *Herbs are so diverse in shape and color that they deserve a garden to themselves, although it need not be classically formal and restrained, as this kitchen herb garden reveals.*

USEFUL UMBELLIFERS

Fennel is a typical umbelliferous herb, with a branching stem system and flattened umbels – heads of little flowers – which are followed by long, aromatic seeds. Many other members of the Umbelliferae family are useful plants, including herbs such as European sweet cicely (Myrrhis odorata), parsley, chervil and angelica, vegetables such as carrots and parsnips, and medicinal herbs such as asafoetida. Unfortunately, some close relatives are extremely toxic – poisonous hemlock is perhaps the most notorious, but there are also others – so it is unwise to gather umbellifers from the wild without accurate identification.

flowers and shrubs for brilliance of color, but their worth lies in their effectiveness as teas, tonics and ointments, for their fragrance, and for the complex flavors they impart to other foods. They are also easier to tend than most choice ornamentals.

USEFUL WEEDS

The nineteenth-century American writer Ralph Waldo Emerson defined a weed as 'a plant whose virtues have not yet been discovered', which is fairer than the common assumption that weeds are unwelcome plants. All plants should be judged by the same criteria, and if they have a pleasing appearance and known virtues they merit room in the herb garden. Wild chamomile, for example, used to be known as the 'plants' physician' for its ability to revive ailing plants nearby, while alliums such as wild garlic and Welsh onions are companion plants for roses, which seem healthier in their presence. Common comfrey has pretty purple flowers, and can be harvested as a compost activator and remedy for skin ailments, while even the ubiquitous chickweed is a valuable salad ingredient with some tonic properties.

There is little difference between garden weeds and wild flowers other than where they grow. Many wayside plants deserve to be grown in gardens, being attractive enough to stand beside cultivated plants, and able to guard them from the threat of pollution and loss of habitat.

HERBS AND WILDLIFE

Bees, butterflies and other wild creatures depend on an enormous selection of plants for their survival. Herbs are ideal conservation plants because their strong perfumes and simple flowers attract browsing insects. In particular, bees love the sweet-scented blooms of thyme, sage, lavender, bergamot, mint, hyssop and rosemary, and it is no coincidence that a beehive was often the centerpiece of medieval herb gardens. Not only butterflies but also hoverflies, whose larvae are voracious allies in controlling pests, enjoy open single flowers or herbs with flat heads of blossom, such as sedum, catmint, sweet rocket and purple loosestrife.

A Place in the Garden

Visiting herb gardens is the best way to decide on which plants to choose and where to grow them. If they are primarily intended for use, it may be enough to gather your favorite kinds in a small accessible bed, which might be a cook's garden of basic culinary herbs, a formally arranged medicinal border, or a relaxed collection of dye herbs in cottage garden style. Some of the more colorful herbs can be planted among ornamental flowers rather than kept separate in a distinct herb garden, while culinary varieties blend happily with kitchen garden crops.

*Chironia
centaurium*

Whatever your intentions, the cultural needs and habits of your plants must come first. It is no good trying to grow a majestic woodland herb such as angelica or lovage in a small, neat bed, for it will dominate the other plants and look hopelessly out of scale. Strictly geometrical designs must be created from evergreen perennials with similar heights and growth rates if the pattern is not to lose its clean outlines or disappear in winter.

Remember, too, that some herbs are very choosy about the soil and aspect they need, whereas others are almost infinitely adaptable – rosemary, for example, thrives almost anywhere, except in cold winters, and may be clipped as an informal flowering hedge or into simple evergreen topiary. A tall variety such as 'Fastigiatus' ('Miss Jessop's Variety') left to grow naturally will grace any shrub border and even support a small clematis for

variety; semi-prostrate 'Severn Sea' is perfect for cascading over a bank; while 'Tuscan Blue' or 'Majorca' with neater growth and brighter flowers are ideal as multi-purpose culinary, medic-

Below: *Whether your garden is a large expanse of soil and shrubs or a small front patch in front of a city house, herbs can be happily combined to produce an attractive display – space need not be a limiting factor in a herb garden.*

ROYAL PRECEDENT

Far from being a modern phenomenon, collecting aromatic herbs can be traced back as far as ancient Egyptian times. Around 1500 BC, Queen Hatshepsut ordered the mass felling of fig trees in her kingdom to build rafts that were poled up the River Nile for hundreds of miles in search of exotic trees and aromatic herbs for the royal gardens. Sennacherib, son of Sargon II of Assyria, constructed magnificent gardens and planted them with myrrh and other aromatic shrubs collected from the lands of the Hittites. Once gathered they were treasured for their great value, and widely used, traded or offered – the Queen of Sheba, for example, is recorded as taking a present of balsam seeds to King Solomon, and King Gentius of Illyria in the second century AD was renowned for his healing exploits with the roots of *Gentiana lutea,* which was named after him.

inal and ornamental container shrubs for a prominent position on the patio.

FITTING IN THE PLANTS

Unless you plan to assemble a comprehensive herb collection immediately, perhaps arranged in classically formal beds, it is best to begin with the few herbs you know you will use constantly, and add others later. Your own needs and preferences must decide which herbs to select, while experience will reveal whether they thrive in the chosen situation. A start could be

Below: *A robust flamboyant climber with ornamental leaves and interesting 'cones' in autumn, the hop plant earns a place in the less formal herb garden as an edible, medicinal and aromatic plant.*

made with essential culinary herbs, planted together in the vegetable garden, leaving until later the option of expanding the collection and moving plants to a dedicated site elsewhere. Most simply, individual herbs may be tucked into existing beds and borders to make their gently colorful contributions, providing an effective foil for brilliant herbaceous plants.

Herbs are irresistibly collectable, however, and finding room for later acquisitions is often a problem, especially in a small garden. A score or so of essential varieties will grow comfortably in a bed about 10 x 3 ft in size, especially if annuals and invasive kinds are confined to containers. Enclosing the bed with a tapestry hedge of evergreens that tolerate clipping permits the addition of hyssop, germander, lavender and similar herbs, while at their base dwarf prostrate kinds (such as pennyroyal, thrift and woolly thyme) can be allowed to billow over the edge of the path. Instead of hedging, you could surround the garden with rustic fencing to support a rose

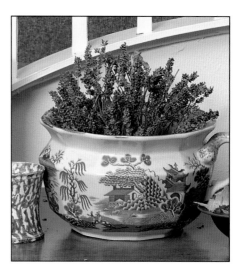

Above: *Aromatic herbs such as thyme and lavender arranged around the house as dried flowers or pot-pourri make inexpensive and efficient air fresheners, combining the ancient tradition of strewing herbs with modern principles of aromatherapy.*

such as 'Zéphirine Drouhin', which is early to flower and one of the last to finish. Fastigiate (slim and upright) or standard shrub varieties can be added to the bed as an extra tier above ground-level plants.

If your ambitions extend further, you may want to consider planting a larger border or separate herb garden. Collections in botanic gardens are often arranged systematically according to use or family, and these will give you an idea of the amount of room needed. Less congenial parts of the garden may be ideal for larger numbers of herbs – a dry bank, for example, is the perfect site for a collection of thymes, an arrangement of decorative pots in a courtyard might house some of the many available kinds of mint in partial shade or basil in full sun, while a simple heap of rubble and soil could be transformed into a herbal rock garden of mat-forming varieties and dwarf shrubs.

Different Types of Herb Garden

Herbs have always been an important ingredient of domestic country gardens, where they were grown almost exclusively for their practical uses. It is only comparatively recently that the cottage garden has been appreciated and become fashionable. Classic cottage garden herbs include the essential culinary species, perhaps with the addition of coriander, garlic and one or two specimens of southernwood or curry plant to brush in passing. On the whole, the authentic range of cottage herbs was fairly conservative.

Veratrum viride

Most herbs can be grown informally, even 'muddled up' with other plants as the garden designer Vita Sackville-West (1892-1962) preferred them to be, although this should not mean total neglect. Like any other plant, herbs become straggly and unkempt if left to themselves or if they seed themselves too liberally among their neighbours, and it is important to keep them in their place by pruning, division, dead-heading or harvesting as necessary.

Some species blend remarkably well into a flowering border, especially more robust kinds such as angelica, foxglove, and bronze fennel which partners prettily the broad leaves of irises and the rich autumn shades of helenium, dwarf sunflowers or rudbeckias. Rue, santolina and lemon balm succeed in the middle of borders, while sage, marjoram, violets and lady's mantle are compact plants for growing near the front.

Annual and biennial herbs can be sown *in situ* or transplanted from elsewhere to fill space in beds and borders. Try sowing pinches of dill, borage, parsley and marigold seeds in pots for emergency use where gaps appear, and add young marjoram, savory and feverfew plants to edgings of pinks and other low perennials. Container-grown mints such as *Mentha* x *gentilis* (ginger mint) and *M. suaveolens* 'Variegata' (pineapple mint) may be plunged into the soil, with the pots buried up to their rims, to fill gaps with their decorative seasonal foliage.

FORMAL GARDENS

Herbs lend themselves most to a formal layout, as they have done since, in Tudor times, gardeners translated embroidery and plaster ceiling patterns into floral designs for the garden. The discipline imposed by a geometrical arrangement of beds and paths has its advantages: the plants are easy to reach for maintenance and harvest, their numerous and complementary shades and shapes are particularly suitable for combining in artistic patterns, and symmetry is satisfying for its own sake.

Designs can be simple and intimate: the familiar fan or cartwheel, for example, with wedge-shaped beds radiating from a common center, or a checkerboard arrangement of alternate paving slabs and square beds, perhaps with small vegetables and salad herbs to

Above: *Even a simple area of stone setts can be transformed into a miniature herb pavement when the joints are planted with prostrate mints, thymes, marjoram and similar mat-forming species.*

Left: *The clean classical outlines of dwarf hedges and evergreen topiary echo the restraint and balanced patterns of a formal herb garden.*

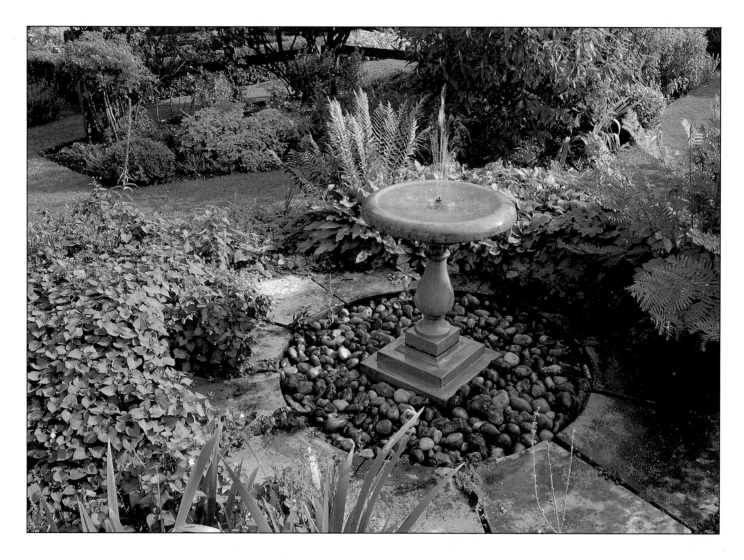

create a French-style *potager;* these are often the most effective, especially in small gardens. Where there is space, larger and more complex gardens are traditional, with beds of herbs surrounded by clipped dwarf hedges of germander, santolina, hyssop or box, either as strict frames for herb parterres or woven and intertwined to produce the classic knot garden.

Precision is essential for ambitious designs to succeed, as is frequent maintenance to keep the hedges trim. Within the chosen framework, herbs can be planted informally in whatever way pleases the eye, arranging them systematically so that culinary herbs are kept separate from medicinal species, for example, or in traditional style, using large numbers of a few compatible herbs to create a form of carpet bedding.

THE WILD HERB GARDEN

The opposite of the strict parterre, a wild herb garden combines informality with the pleasures of re-creating a natural environment and providing a haven for wildlife. The ground needs to be prepared in the same way as for conventional herb borders, because there will be room only for chosen plants and not for some of the more invasive wild species. Arrange naturally meandering paths, together with one or two places to sit in peace and, if possible, a pool for moisture-loving herbs and aquatic wildlife. There is no need to level the ground – in fact, banks, hollows and gentle undulations add to the garden's

Above: *Many herbs have a natural exuberance that makes them ideal for herbaceous borders and wild gardens. These informal beds border a cool turf path beside which a strategically placed pedestal fountain plays.*

charm. Choose seeds of herbal wild flowers, grasses and woodland herbs such as angelica, woodruff, campion and lovage (some specialist seedsmen will blend a mixture to your requirements), and sow at the appropriate time. Add ferns, and a few suitable shrubs and trees such as elder, crab apple or quince. The only maintenance necessary will be routine cutting back to restrain vigorous species, the removal of unwelcome species, and occasional propagation of older perennials.

The Ornamental Herb Garden

Bryonia cretica

Although individual herbs may look their best when in flower or in early spring as the young foliage unfolds, a decorative herb garden can be expected to give pleasure at every season, and year-round interest should be taken into account when drawing up garden plans. Include some hardy evergreen species to balance the seasonal changes and to provide winter color and continuity from one year to the next: variegated and colored forms remain brilliant highlights on even the darkest days.

Herbaceous herbs die down to the ground as the season closes, leaving areas of bare ground, so be sure to disperse evergreens to provide plenty of attractive ground cover in spite of winter gaps in your design.

Some perennial herbs take time to get started in spring, but early color is provided by groups and drifts of bulbs such as winter aconites, snowdrops and early crocuses. Hardy annuals sown in pots or in a frame in autumn

flower earlier than those sown outdoors, and they can be hardened off for transplanting where there is space in the herb garden. Later sowings of annuals provide a succession of color throughout the season.

Height is an essential consideration in any design, for many herbs are small to medium-sized plants and on their own may give a herb garden a disappointing uniformity. A feature such as a sundial, statue or large urn can relieve the flatness, although you should always consider the scale of the garden and the suitability of any ornaments – they must neither dominate nor spoil the overall impact of the design. A central feature is traditional, or you could embellish corners and turns in paths with smaller features – but guard against triviality, for it is easy to destroy the elegance of a herb garden with banal additions.

Topiary is another classic means of providing height, and several herbal plants adapt readily to formal

Left: *An inspired choice of striking colors and leaf forms will produce a memorable display, and proves that herbs are not only useful and practical plants, but also as decorative as any summer bedding.*

clipping. Common yew, holly, rosemary and bay where hardy, lavender and larger forms of box are ideal for bold designs that will catch the eye all the year round. Trained plants such as honeysuckle on pillars and standard or weeping roses are all suitable for hedges, and need little attention apart from annual pruning and tying in to supporting frames. On a larger scale, arches clad with climbers, tunnels of trained fruit, vines or hops, and even substantial pergolas of brick and timber can be used to frame paths or emphasize paved areas. For shade, some of the more ornamental trees with herbal connotations can be planted – elder, almond, cherry, quince, juniper or walnut, for example, according to the space available.

At least one seat is essential for prolonged peaceful enjoyment of the herb garden, especially in the evening when colors and scents are most intense. Position it where you are likely to sit most often, perhaps at the far end or facing your favorite view. There is a wide choice of styles and materials for garden seats, from elegantly wrought iron to simple rustic timber, or you can construct a bank from mounded earth, covering it with turf, thyme or chamomile around a stone or timber slab for all-weather seating; add a few plants of heartsease (wild pansy) and primrose for Shakespearean authenticity. Plant one or two aromatic herbs nearby to scent the area, and for intimacy train fragrant roses and honeysuckle on a framework arching over the seat to form a secluded arbor.

BUILDING A HERB WHEEL

1 *Mark out the planned area, using a peg and taut line to ensure a perfect circle, before removing the turf and some of the topsoil. Ideally, the subsoil should also be loosened.*

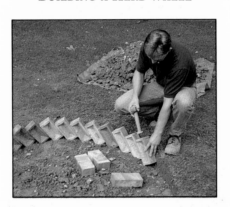

2 *Position the edging materials, here house bricks arranged at an oblique angle and tapped firmly into place, but special-purpose edging tiles would be more frost-resistant.*

3 *Quarter the circle with two courses of sound bricks to allow access and create four separate beds.*

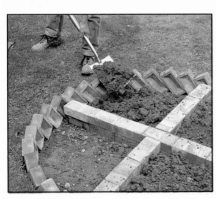

4 *Break up the excavated topsoil and refill the four quadrants almost to the surface of the brick paths.*

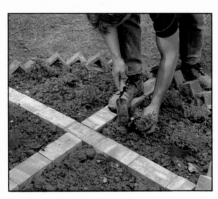

5 *Plant pot-grown herbs of your choice, watering them beforehand and allowing enough room for expansion as they grow.*

6 *Water in the plants if necessary, and then mulch with gravel or chippings to retain moisture and suppress weeds.*

Herbs for Color

It is sometimes claimed that herbs are not sufficiently varied to create an interesting garden by themselves, but this is not so. Even if only green varieties are used, rather than variegated forms, there are so many leaf shapes and contrasting plant habits in an infinity of green shades that a satisfying composition can be made from basic species alone.

Malva sylvestris

Green is, after all, a color like any other, and green forms are particularly welcome in winter when evergreen herbs supply color while all around seems dormant, as noted by Thomas Hyll in 1563 in *The Art of Gardening*, where he advised that knot gardens should be 'set with winter savory and thyme, for these endure all the winter through greene'.

Achieving a riot of brilliant color with herbs is not easy. Most are subtly colored, low-key plants, which helps explain the healing sense of refreshment and well-being in a herb garden. Vibrant, exciting colors are only found in a few flowers and leaves – peonies and poppies, nasturtiums, golden elders and the ruby Pasque flower, for example. Many variegated leaves have a brilliance of their own, however, especially if grown in full sun. Always assess plants before you buy them, because some forms, gold variations in particular, can be confused with normal plants suffering from a mosaic virus.

Color needs to be used with discretion in the herb garden, where strident exuberance is usually out of place. Carefully position single specimens of brightly colored plants as important accents or to mark entrances, exits and changes in the layout – remember that a dominant color only works by contrast with its surroundings, and the more subdued plants should predominate for maximum effect. They may be paler, for example a sea of silver santolinas, set off with a few bobbing red poppies; or more somber, such as the dark foliage of a yew hedge as a background for bright yellow mullein.

The low-toned colors of most herbs work best in simple designs, such as the contrast between woven green box and grey lavender hedges in a knot garden, or variations on monochrome planting made popular by the garden

Above: *Formal geometrical designs are best planted in blocks of contrasting colors and leaf shapes for the greatest impact, using sculptural highlights such as simple topiary to relieve any uniformity.*

NOTABLE HERB FLOWERS

- borage – rich blue, for salads and summer drinks
- lavender – soft purple, for scent and pot-pourri
- nasturtiums – vivid reds and yellows, for colored garnishes
- violets – purple, for medicines and crystallized as decoration
- elderflowers – white and fragrant, for wines, cordials, and flavoring fruit dishes
- pot marigolds or calendulas – vivid orange, for salads, pot-pourri and food coloring
- rose petals – red roses of scented varieties, for color and fragrance, wines and perfume
- woodruff – tiny and white, imparts scent of hay and vanilla when warm

designer Gertrude Jekyll (1843-1932), who created cool blue and grey borders and sunny yellow gardens. True blues are hard to find among herbs, though there are blue-flowered species such as chicory, borage, flax, hyssop, lavender and sea holly. However, there are many subtle shades of lilac and violet which harmonize with the greys and silvers of lavender, artemisia and rue. Yellows and golds are easier to mass, for these colors form the majority of variegations. Most herbs have forms with white leaves or flowers (cultivar names such as 'Alba', 'Alba Plena' and 'Albovariegata' are indications of these), and a white garden, at the same time cool and reviving, is perhaps the most popular of single-color themes.

Herbs in the red, purple and brown part of the spectrum are hardest to use effectively. Depending on the quality of light and surrounding plants, they can look rich and sumptuous, or merely lackluster. Deep red forms make excellent groundwork and specimen plants: crimson or purple bugle, for example, beneath the soft green of lady's mantle, or red

Above left: *Planted in drifts, flowering herbs such as wall germander can erupt into a startling carpet of color that will be alive with bees in summer.*

Right: *A branch of wild marjoram in full bloom reveals an intensity of color to rival any decorative shrub.*

Above right: *Ornamental forms of edible herbs add a decorative bonus to the salad garden: French sorrel (*Rumex scutatus*), for example, has the same tangy flavor as ordinary sorrel, but also creates a carpet of ground-cover foliage.*

sage (*Salvia officinalis* 'Purpurescens') standing out against a carpet of pale golden marjoram. Remember, though, that reds change as the day progresses and in full sun can reach out towards you, whereas evening twilight makes them recede almost to the point of invisibility.

FOLIAGE BEDS

When designing herb beds and borders, do not sacrifice leaf shape to color, for the two qualities work together and can blend to make a stun-

ning impact. The many thistle-like herbs are spectacularly eye-catching, creating dramatic stands of green, grey or silver foliage and robust stems: holy thistles, cardoons, globe artichokes, sea holly and milk thistles are all plants of great presence. Ferns, too, form a group with wide design potential, especially as a number of them have intricately varied forms with ruffled, divided or filigree detail. Their shades vary, and they tolerate moist shade, offering scope for planting schemes in corners where little else will flourish.

Herbs for Fragrance

*Until the reign of King George IV (1820-30) English monarchs appointed
Strewers of Herbs to precede them in procession and scatter dried aromatic herbs
such as rosemary, thyme and rue to ward off diseases. The appointment of these
royal 'strewing ladies', as they were popularly known, was a legacy from the times
of the medieval plagues, which were thought to be caused by foul air. Dried herbs
and essential oils were incorporated into pot-pourris, snuff, fumigants and
scented waters, in the belief that fragrance would deter both infections and
insects; and judges still carry posies of sweet herbs to shield themselves from the
rest of humanity in the courtroom.*

Anthemis nobilis

Research has shown that there is some substance to medieval ideas of hygiene. While most plants attract insects, others actively repel them. Others have an antiseptic effect, for example the gums exuded by some trees to heal wounds in their bark. These varied effects of fragrance have become part of the great tradition of herbal use, but in garden terms perfume is usually regarded as one of the pleasant qualities of desirable plants, especially herbs. Plant fragrances are hard to describe precisely. They are traditionally classified, simply by nose, in groups such as camphoraceous, fruity or hay-scented. Some scents, most notably those of open flowers (roses and gardenias, for example), are released as a reaction to sunshine – most of the Mediterranean herbs protect themselves from prolonged heat by surrounding their foliage with a defensive cloud of volatile oils.

Night-flowering plants often have heavy scents, and plants such as honeysuckle, nicotiana and evening primrose should be grown near an open window or beside a seat where you can enjoy their fragrance on a still evening. Plants that flower in winter also need planting close at hand for appreciation in all weathers. Disperse others according to the strength of their fragrance: the heady scent of *Lilium regale* can fill large areas and reach you from far away, whereas other plants need close approach to be enjoyed, and should therefore be placed within easy reach.

Left: *The smoky blue foliage of rue has a
sharply resinous pungency, and a
reputation for causing skin irritations if
carelessly handled.*

Drying lavender: 1 *Heads of lavender flowers gathered at the peak of their perfection. Timing is important, and for full fragrance the flowers should be gathered when fully opened, whereas for medicinal use the critical time is often just before flowering.*

2 Spread out the complete flowering shoots to dry, in the sun or in shade according to species, or in warmth indoors in a cool season (lavender is best dried in a shady room). Turn the flowers frequently to ensure that all parts are dried.

3 The complete flowering shoots can be used intact, or individual blooms can be stripped off when dry for use in pot-pourri, herb bags and sachets. Keep different varieties separate, as their perfumes will be subtly different.

Leaf scents tend to be released when the foliage is bruised or brushed in passing, and most culinary herbs fall into this category, as well as aromatic trees and shrubs such as eucalyptus, rosemary, southernwood and the resinous conifers. Plant them strategically beside seats, at corners in paths or flanking gateways. Many of these species also make excellent hedges, and in earlier times it was the custom to spread freshly washed clothes on hedges to absorb a little of their fragrance while they dried.

Drying herbs often enhances their scent, sometimes releasing it from otherwise insignificant herbs – the delicious hayfield fragrance of sweet woodruff only reaches its full intensity days after the plant is cut and hung to dry, for example. Essential oils and tinctures are prepared from many herbs for use in aromatherapy or as Bach homeopathic flower remedies, where particular fragrances have been found to heal disorders and change moods. In the garden, plants can have the similar effect of raising your spirits or soothing tension, so be sure to plant your favorite scented herbs where they are accessible when needed.

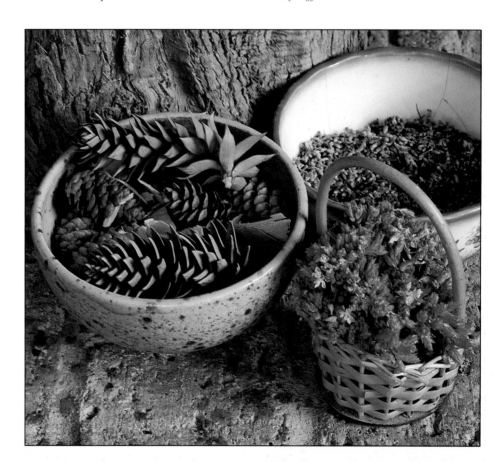

Above: *The most important feature of pot-pourri is its fragrance, so ingredients such as thyme and lavender must be dried thoroughly to concentrate the volatile oils.*

Right: *Carpeting herbs such as chamomile, thyme and pennyroyal are ideal ground cover plants for informal lawns, which give off a heady scent when walked upon.*

Herbs for Clipping

The more you clip a woody perennial, the denser the foliage becomes: this is the principle behind hedge trimming, topiary and mowing lawns. Really a form of pruning, trimming off the end of a stem usually encourages the development of two or more side shoots, and the best species for hedges and lawns are those that respond to clipping by producing the densest regrowth.

Gratiola officinalis

Compact plants such as rosemary, lavender, santolina, southern-wood, germander, hyssop, yew and, of course, box are traditional for herb garden hedges ranging in height from 6 in around small beds to 6 ft 6 in in grander schemes. Their chief function is to enclose, divide or define herb borders, conferring a sense of order and control, but they can be used to create the playful patterns of classic knot gardens and are often decorative in their own right, especially when kept neatly disciplined – this requires only one, perhaps two, trims a year in the case of box and yew, but vigorous plants such as privet and lonicera need clipping every month during the growing season.

Lavender is a particular favorite for a herb hedge and will yield a generous supply of flowers and leaves for dry-ing. Use a compact cultivar rather than the loose-growing English and trailing forms, and clip it to shape in spring without cutting into the old wood; leave it to flower and then trim it again, harvesting the fading blooms for use. In warm gardens, santolina's intricate silver foliage is a useful foil for green plants, and if it is trimmed close in mid-spring it will retain its neat shape, although the yellow button-shaped flowers will be sacrificed.

Frequently clipped hedges make special demands on the soil, and the site should therefore be well dug beforehand, at the same time adding plenty of compost or decayed manure to sustain fast growth. Clear perennial weeds as you work, for these are hard to remove afterwards, and always plant in single rather than staggered rows to allow access for weeding in the early years before the hedge is established. Water the hedge thoroughly in dry weather during its first year or two, and feed it annually because you want to encourage rapid development in both height and density, together with prompt revival after clipping, which must start at an early age.

Topiary needs the same kind of thoughtful preparation and care, for it is no more than a whimsical form of hedge training and clipping. Used for ornament since Roman times, it can have a dramatic impact, especially where specimens are given positions of prominence – a mop-head bay in the centre of a herb garden, box finials to embellish the corners of beds, or rosemary obelisks as sentinels beside gateways and paths, for example. Feed and water topiary regularly, and clip it frequently with scissors to maintain the shape. Use plants sparingly and with discretion: you are creating a herb garden, not an exhibition of topiary, and they should serve only as decorative highlights.

HERB LAWNS

Prostrate herbs are suitable for growing densely to create fragrant lawns that can be kept neat, preferably after flowering in most cases, by clipping with shears or mowing with the mower

HERBS FOR POTTED TOPIARY

- germander
- mintbush (*Prostanthera rotundifolia*)
- rosemary
- scented-leaf pelargoniums (especially *P. crispum*)
- manuka (*Leptospermum scoparium*)
- myrtle – especially *Myrtus communis* 'Microphylla'
- santolina (including *S. virens*)
- Victorian rosemary

blades set high. They are not as hard-wearing as turf and therefore should be made in corners of their own or where traffic is not heavy, but they have a special timeless charm and surround you with fragrance when you tread on them.

A lawn made of chamomile is traditional – use a non-flowering clone such as 'Treneague' – and it has the advantage of remaining green long after drought has scorched ordinary turf. It can be difficult to keep weed-free, however, requires shearing rather than mowing, and after only a few years usually needs remaking; it is better planted in mortar joints between paving slabs where it is more easily maintained. Thyme (single or contrasting variegated cultivars) and mint-scented pennyroyal are far more satisfactory lawn herbs, producing thick mats of growth that once established suppress most weeds, and both bear heavy flushes of attractive flowers as a bonus.

To make a herb lawn, the ground needs thorough preparation in the same way as a seedbed, with a top dressing of general fertilizer raked in just before planting. Plant your lawn in

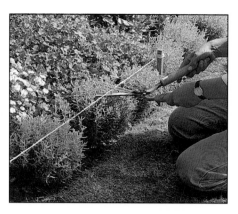

Above left: *Even while young and still growing, hedging herbs, such as santolina, need clipping to induce bushy growth.*

Above right: *A taut line acts as a guide and helps ensure consistent height and width along the hedge.*

spring or autumn, setting chamomile plants about 4 in apart, other species at 12 in spacings, and water it well until it is established. Chamomile spreads faster if it is occasionally rolled (Shakespeare's Falstaff noticed, 'The more it is trodden on the better it grows'). Remove any weeds promptly before they get a hold, especially in the early stages while there is still bare soil to colonize.

Above: *Many grey and silver herbs, such as santolina, can be kept neat and compact if clipped in spring and prevented from flowering by a further trim in summer.*

Left: *The traditional knot garden, with its contrasting threads of hedging plants, takes several seasons before it is established, and the small plants from which it develops need frequent clipping to transform them into dense hedges.*

Herbs as Flowering Plants

Visually the flowering season is a pinnacle of delight in the herb garden. Although herbs cannot compete with the gaudiness of summer bedding plants, their soft and subtle flower hues contribute a cottage garden innocence, altogether in keeping with their sensuous simplicity. Many of the flowers are useful in their own right, for their fragrance and color in pot-pourri, their medicinal uses in cosmetics and tisanes, or simply for eating in salads and adding to cool summer drinks.

Althaea officiualis

It is a mistake to assume that herbs are grown primarily for their leaves, and that allowing them to bloom exhausts their energies or dilutes their active properties. The removal of flowers is only occasionally necessary: strictly formal hedges lose their precise geometry if allowed to bloom, and annuals such as basil will deteriorate rapidly after flowering. Prolific self-seeders, such as fennel and angelica, need dead-heading for restraint, or you can cut out the flowering stems at an earlier stage.

Many herbs have a rich tradition of religious or national symbolism: the chrysanthemum in China and Japan, for example, and jasmine in Arab

ENCOURAGING HONEY BEES

If you keep honey bees yourself or find that large numbers regularly visit your garden, planting some of their favourite flowers (not necessarily the same as those frequented by bumble bees) will increase the honey flow or entice them to stay and fertilize your fruit and vegetable crops.

- basil
- borage
- clover
- crocus
- hollyhock
- ivy
- lemon balm
- marjoram
- mustard
- rosemary
- savory
- bergamot
- bugle
- comfrey
- dandelion
- hyssop
- lavender
- mallow
- mint
- pulmonaria
- sage
- thyme

cultures, and as early as the second century AD the Greek *Dream Book of Artimedorus* catalogued the meanings attached to flowers. A large number were sacred to the Virgin Mary – hence the profusion of common names prefixed with 'Mary', 'lady', and 'Our Lady's' – and these were often gathered in medieval St Mary Gardens.

Left: *Feverfew, like other members of the Compositae family such as chamomile and tansy, has pretty daisy-like flowers which are as medicinally useful as its leaves.*

Elizabethan floral alphabets and the Victorian love of creating bouquets of flowers to send floral messages are all part of this enduring tradition. Even herbal weeds and wild flowers had their significance: chickweed meant you wanted to make a rendezvous, buttercups promised prosperity and sorrel affection, while the course of love could be charted with foxglove for treachery and hops for injustice, followed inevitably by evening primrose for uncertainty, lily of the valley for restored joy and finally rosemary for remembrance.

Herbs for seeds

Flowering leads ultimately to seeding, an important part of the herbal calendar, as many plants are cultivated for their seeds, sometimes exclusively: caraway, coriander, cumin, dill, fenugreek, mustard, poppy and sesame are all staple seed producers. Where large quantities are needed, plants are best grown as utility crops in the kitchen garden, perennials gathered in a sunny corner and annuals sown in rows between the vegetables, for few seeding herbs look very decorative, and you will probably want to prevent accidental seeding among other herbs. Always choose a warm position for them, to help seeds ripen and dry on the plants.

Useful garden flowers

In addition to familiar herbs with attractive blooms, there are plants that are normally grown for ornament in flower beds and borders, but which have traditional herbal uses, and these provide valuable extra color in the herb garden. Larger species, such as eucalyptus, elder, broom, hollyhock and mullein, all contribute height as well as color. For the middle of borders, you can integrate blue cornflowers, sea holly, greater celandine (beware of self-seeding), peonies, columbines and hydrangeas, while the edges of beds are ideal for low-growing plants such as thrift, candytuft, violets and garden pinks.

1 Many flowering herbs can be used to make herbal teas and tisanes. Collect the flowerheads in summer and allow them to dry. Store them in sealed containers so that they keep well. To make a tea, place 1 tbsp dried flowers or petals per person in a teapot or jug and fill with boiling water.

2 Leave the infusion to steep for 5-8 minutes. When the flavor is strong enough, pour slowly through a strainer.

Left: *The prolific heads of arching borage flowers self-seed freely and guarantee plenty of seedlings for the next year. The ample crop of blooms can also be floated in summer drinks, face-upwards to display their immaculate shape and intense violet-blue color.*

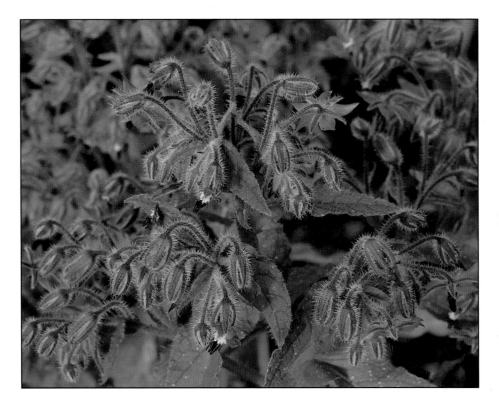

Salad Herbs

People have gathered herbs for thousands of years, not just in their search for natural remedies, but also to supplement their diet with nutritious wild plants. Lettuce, cabbage and carrots are all derived from wild ancestors that sometimes bear little obvious resemblance to their modern descendants. Few people today would want to depend on these primitive plants for their food, but numerous wild flowers, herbs and even weeds remain popular as salad ingredients, while some are still used occasionally as leaf vegetables or pot herbs for cooking.

Daucus carota

Early salads, or 'sallets' as they were known, seem wildly eclectic in comparison with today's cautious list of limited ingredients, and it is only recently that we are beginning once more to include the vast larder of herbal flavors. In the late seventeenth century, John Evelyn was already complaining about the impoverished imagination of contemporary cooks, compared with the Latin races 'who gather anything almost that is tender to the very tops of nettles, so as every Hedge affords a sallet (not una-greeable), and seasoned with Vinegar Salt and Oil, which gives it both the relish and the name of Salad…'.

It must be added that gathering wild herbs indiscriminately has its very real dangers, as Evelyn observed when he reminded us that 'Sad experience shows how many fatal mistakes have been made by those who took hemlock for aconite, cow weed for Chervil, Dog's Mercury for Spinach, whose dire effects have been many times sudden death and the cause of mortal accidents…'.

The best way to avoid 'mortal accidents' is to grow salad herbs in the garden where their identity is known. Even then it is wise to use only moderate amounts, for many are pungent or strongly flavored and are added sparingly for a hint of stimulating flavor, while the most benign herb can have unforeseen effects if taken in large

Above: *Sorrel is particularly welcome in early spring, when it supplies tasty and nutritious leaves long before conventional salad ingredients are ready. Lamb's lettuce is another useful hardy leaf herb.*

Left: *Garlic chives, like other alliums, are valuable members of the salad herb garden, combining culinary usefulness with all the charm of delicate wild flowers.*

quantities: over-consumption of parsley, for example, has been known to cause liver damage.

Nevertheless, a leaf taken from here and there, together with a few colored edible flowers, will add interest and piquancy to a plain salad, and there is every reason to revive the flair and variety of older traditions. Growing your favourite salad ingredients together in a separate bed will create an attractive miniature garden that can be harvested easily, for it need only take a few minutes to gather leaves of various lettuces, burnet, dandelion, fennel, lovage, lemon balm, common daisy and pulmonaria, together with flowers such as marigolds, cowslips, violets, nasturtiums and bugloss for a connoisseur's salad. Chinese cabbage is an ideal substitute for lettuce in oriental salads, especially when mixed with authentic herbs such as sesame seeds, ginger, lemon grass, mugwort and mallow.

NATURAL SEEDBEDS

Chervil and parsley, both popular salad herbs, can be grown as self-perpetuating crops, producing their own self-sown seedlings for subsequent use. Simply transfer a single parsley plant to a clear part of a nursery bed, where you can continue using its foliage until it flowers in its second year from sowing. Keep the soil clear around the base of the plant as the seeds ripen, and you will find these fall and produce a bed of seedlings to transplant for future supplies. Chervil behaves in the same way, although as an annual it self-seeds within a single season. It is best sown broadcast in patches, where later generations of seedlings can remain to form a constantly regenerating bed.

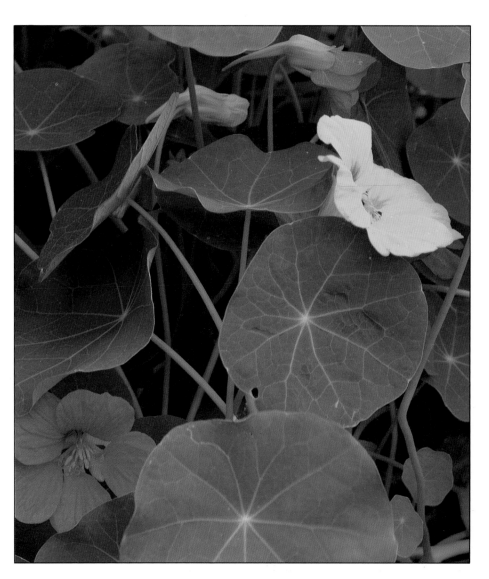

HOP SHOOTS

Apart from their important commercial use as a flavoring and preservative in brewing, hops have medicinal and culinary value, and are also grown as ornamental climbers where space allows. The twining annual stems can reach 20 ft or more on strong supports of posts and wires, their handsome foliage and decorative female 'cones' making them ideal companions for climbing roses to divide larger gardens. From the dormant crowns more shoots emerge in spring than will be needed, so thin them when they are about 6-8 in tall, leaving four to six of the strongest, and steam or poach the surplus shoots as an alternative to asparagus.

Above: *Many familiar flowering annuals make useful additions to a herb collection: nasturtiums not only add a bright splash of color to the garden, but their leaves are edible, the pleasantly flavored flowers can be used to brighten up salads, and the seeds, when pickled, taste very similar to capers.*

Herbs for Seasoning

National cuisines have evolved over many centuries and even now include strong echoes of former customs. The choice of seasoning herbs is no exception. Certain flavors are instantly attributable to regional cookery: sumac, cardamom and sesame in the Middle East, Mediterranean olives, garlic and dill in northern Europe, saffron in North Africa and chillies in Mexico, lemon grass in South-East Asia, ginger and star anise in China, and a multitude of Indian seasonings such as coriander, fenugreek, nigella and turmeric.

Coriandrum sativum

Modern cooks add herbs to a dish for flavoring rather than for medicinal or preservative purposes, but earlier generations used them from necessity. A medieval peasant, for example, often could not afford to feed his livestock through the winter and so would slaughter animals in autumn and keep the meat as best he could. In the days before refrigeration, stored produce gradually deteriorated, and strong flavors, easily provided by herbs, were needed to disguise stale ingredients in a dish.

Apart from the historical reasons for adding them, herbs all serve some further purpose, whether it is to stimulate the appetite, aid digestion or stop the food from going off.

Horseradish is a pungent seasoning with typical antibiotic properties, used for centuries in Europe to preserve meat and disguise 'off' flavors, although the sauce prepared from its roots is now more usually regarded as an optional condiment with roast beef. The plant, which resembles an over-enthusiastic dock, belongs in the safety of the kitchen garden, where it

can be grown as an annual root crop or as a perennial in a confined space to restrain its natural invasiveness. Here, too, you should grow coriander, whether for its seeds or spicy leaves; the sturdy annual fenugreek, undistinguished in appearance but essential for curries; and the various kinds of mustard with their medicinal, seasoning and carminative uses.

DIGESTIVE AIDS

Seasonings primarily satisfy the palate, while carminatives aid later digestion. Several herbs, all important candidates for the culinary herb garden, possess volatile oils that are helpful in preventing wind or stimulating the

MINT ROOT CUTTINGS

1 Mint beds need regular renewal, which is easily done by taking healthy young roots, trimming them into short sections and pressing these into trays of moist compost.

2 Cover the cuttings with a layer of compost, and they will soon start to grow – those prepared in early autumn can provide young shoots for winter use.

Above: *Many culinary herbs blend perfectly together; for bouquets garnis gather the various ingredients at the same time and mix together in small bunches, as they are easier to assemble while fresh.*

secretion of digestive juices, and many people like to include one or two of these at the table. Dill is perhaps best known because of its popularity in the form of dill water or 'gripe water', but caraway, coriander, fennel and aniseed are also effective carminatives, either separately or mixed in equal proportions. The seeds are the part used, so make a point of leaving them to flower for harvesting at the end of the season.

Maintaining supplies

Since gardeners tend to grow herbs mainly for seasoning, it is well worth trying to plan a continuous supply. Most culinary herbs can be preserved by drying or some other method, but in most cases the fresh product has a better flavor. Some kinds can be potted up in autumn or sown in late summer to reach their peak during the winter, and these will often provide useful crops on a kitchen window sill. A warm greenhouse or conservatory is a more congenial home out of season for potted herbs because they receive more light there, but you can also keep many hardy kinds growing in a cold frame by reserving a sequence of pots there until needed. A permanent collection of perennials may be planted in a soil-based frame, while a portable frame can be placed over a specially planted bed in the autumn. Protect individual plants with cloches or smaller covers, and wrap these with old mats or several sheets of bubble wrap in the event of frost.

Herb Oils

1 Herb oils can be used to add flavor to cooked dishes, salad dressings or marinades. Use one large bunch of herb leaves and 1³/₄ pints of olive oil. Take a large bunch of a leafy seasoning herb such as mint or basil and separate the leaves from the stems. Tear the leaves into rough strips and discard the stems.

2 Using a pestle and mortar, pound the leaves with a little of the olive oil to release the flavor, gradually adding more leaves as the first few begin to break up.

3 Half fill a sterilized bottle with olive oil and half of the herb leaves. Add a generous pinch of rock salt and fill the bottle with the remaining oil and leaves. Seal firmly and leave to stand for two weeks, tipping the bottle upside down occasionally to ensure the flavors mix.

Left: *Gather culinary herbs for preserving on a warm, dry day, selecting clean, healthy pieces which can then be tied for drying in bundles, on their own or combined in bouquets.*

Above: *Herbs gathered fresh from the garden provide an instant assortment of flavors. Short sprigs can be snipped using scissors or clippers; use quickly or keep in a jar of water on a window sill for a few hours.*

Right: *Seasoning herbs such as bay, chives, rosemary and parsley are easy to grow and have an excellent flavor when fresh. Try experimenting with different culinary combinations when planning a new herb bed.*

Herbs for Healing

Cedronella triphylla

Herbs have long held an important place in the treatment of ailments, and herbal remedies are still popular. Today, the pace of research is accelerating rapidly throughout the world, using various scientific skills to evaluate plants and native traditions in the search for new remedies.

Homer wrote of healing roots, one of the earliest records of the use of medicinal plants in Europe, but Chinese manuals and Indian Ayurvedic texts pre-date this by centuries. Much early herbal medicine was based on superstition: the 'Doctrine of Signatures', for example, stated that a herb would treat that part of the body which it most resembled. European settlers arriving in North America found that the Indian inhabitants had their own version of the doctrine, and would associate yellow herbs with jaundice or red ones with blood disorders.

Most herbal remedies were compounds extracted and blended by apothecaries from several plants, each of which was known on its own as a 'simple'. Apothecaries realized that there were differences in purity and potency between substances found in similar species, and that the effects also depended on factors such as the site where they were gathered, or the time of the month or year. In an attempt to standardize quality, the first secular gardens of simples were established in Pisa, Padua, and thereafter throughout Europe and elsewhere – the first such garden in North America was planted by Dr John Bartram in Philadelphia in 1782. They were organized along the lines of earlier monastic hospital gardens, and were generally known as 'Physic Gardens'. It was here that systematic study of plants began in earnest, combining the disciplines of botany and medicine.

Very often scientific discoveries are based on established local use. Romanies, peasants and rainforest tribesmen alike have needed to be accurate botanists for their very survival. These people have understood the healing capabilities of plants in skilled hands, but they have also appreciated the potential dangers of misuse: rue was chosen by Mohammed, for example, as the most blessed of all herbs and it is central to many Arab and Chinese therapies, but it contains a number of active princi-

Left: *In the herbal pharmacy, fresh or dried herbs have been prepared for medicinal use for centuries, drawing on the accumulated wisdom and experience of generations of herbalists. Diagnosis and prescription are still best left to a qualified practitioner, although simple remedies can be prepared at home.*

HERB BALM

1 A herb balm can soothe aching muscles and so aid relaxation. Weigh out 1 oz fresh lavender and rosemary stems, mixed.

2 Place the herbs in a small pan set over a bain-marie. Add 1 pint olive or sunflower oil. Cover with a light lid and simmer for 2 hours, adding more water as necessary.

3 Allow to cool slightly then strain the liquid into a clean bowl.

4 Leave the liquid to cool and then pour into a sterilized jar or bottle and seal. Apply sparingly.

ples which often cause sensitivity to light, and people often develop skin rashes after contact with the plant.

Herbs interact in complex ways with our body chemistry, and their power to heal is formidable. Compared with synthetic drugs their actions may seem very mild, but you should not underestimate the dangers of self-medication on the assumption that herbs are harmless. Many traditional remedies are based on fantasy, guesswork and suggestion, while even the most reputable herbs are selective in their effects, working for one patient but not another.

Only a trained practitioner is qualified to diagnose an ailment, and then to suggest a personal prescription after fully assessing your individual needs. The medical benefits of herbs are no longer in doubt, and many are generally quite safe, provided that they are not misused or taken in circumstances

Right: *It is not just the visible flowers and leaves of herbs that are valuable. Very often the fresh or dried roots, such as those of comfrey, contain the highest concentrations of active ingredients.*

where allergic reactions or side effects are possible – even garlic, widely regarded as an infallible panacea, may reduce blood pressure and so cancel the impact of drugs taken for cardiac disorders. All the plants are complex factories producing diverse chemicals, some of them fragrances to attract pollinating insects, others toxins to deter predators, and any one of these substances may be harmful in particular circumstances.

NATURAL INSECTICIDES

Many plants produce natural insecticides as part of their defence systems, and some of these are widely used as prepared powders and liquids in the garden. Derris, or rotenone, a popular insecticide approved for organic use, is extracted from the powdered roots of a Malaysian shrub known as tuba root (*Derris elliptica*).

Sometimes particular species are grown as companion plants to protect crops nearby from attack.

Various *Tagetes* species have been found to repel whitefly and other pests when grown in greenhouses, and scientific experiments now confirm that their flowers emit volatile chemicals into the surrounding air for protection. As these have proved toxic to the mosquitoes that carry malaria and yellow fever, it is hoped that a new generation of insecticides can be developed for their control.

Herbs for Dyeing

Anyone who has gathered wild blackberries in autumn or pinched out sideshoots from tomato plants will readily appreciate the possibilities of using plant stains to dye animal skins and woven material. Until chemical dyes were introduced, roots, bark, flowers and leaves were the chief sources of color, often made permanent by the addition of mordants – fixing chemicals – from mineral-rich earths and other sources. The shades obtained are rarely vivid, but mellow, subtle, and full of the lustrous beauty of the plants themselves.

Urtica dioica

Ancient China, India and other Asian countries developed sophisticated skills in dyeing, but similar techniques have always been used by tribespeople around the world, who adapted plant materials for painting on bark, to ornament clothing or decorate the skin in preparation for religious ceremonies or warfare, and even for disguise – Romanies once artificially tanned their faces with juices obtained from a favourite herb, *Lycopus europaeus* or gipsywort. The early Britons were described by Julius Caesar as 'blue and terrible' after they had dyed their skin with woad to make their appearance more alarming, while in ancient Egypt the plant was also used to color imperial garments.

Dyeing with herbs remains a popular and pleasant craft, although large amounts of material are often needed, and colors tend to fade gently unless made fast with chemical mordants such as alum, tin, iron or chrome. Results vary according to the strength of the dye, the length of time that the wool (the easiest material to color) is left immersed, and the parts of a plant that are used: the leaves of privet, for example, give yellow shades, whereas the berries impart a muted blue-green hue.

Some plants can be gathered from the wild, but in view of the amounts needed there is the risk of over-

Above: *Woad, or dyer's rocket, is cultivated in many countries for its distinctive blue dye.*

Left: *Manufacture of indigo dye paste from a species of* Indigofera *in southwest China.*

harvesting species that may not be abundant, and it is often better to grow your own supplies of the more useful kinds in a special dye border. This can be an attractive feature, for many of the plants are popular garden ornamentals whose flowers or fruits are the parts used, so that geraniums, dahlias, rudbeckia and mulberries can earn a place as dye plants in the herb garden. Experiment with various leaves after pruning or clipping shrubs and hedges, as many will impart various shades of yellow and green.

CLASSIC DYE CROPS

Traditional dye plants worth growing include the ancient woad (*Isatis tinctoria*), a leafy spinach-like plant whose use dwindled rapidly after the introduction of the more permanent blue dye from the indigo plant, *Indigofera tinctoria*, a subtropical species which needs to be grown in a warm greenhouse in temperate regions.

Dyer's madder (*Rubia tinctorum*) is a self-seeding perennial still cultivated

Above: *Woolen yarn dyed using homegrown* Polygonum tinctorum. *Shades are varied by the number of immersions in the vat.*

Right: *Indigo plants,* Strobilanthes flaccidifolius, *growing in a field in Guizhou Province, south-west China. Plants are cultivated annually from cuttings – the precursor of the dye is contained in the leaves.*

on a field scale in France and the Netherlands, and an important European source of strong red, while in North America bloodroot (*Sanguinaria canadensis*) was the main plant used by Indians for red body paint. Weld (*Reseda luteola*) (or dyer's greenweed, *Genista tinctoria*), a relative of broom, another dye source, is a traditional yellow dye plant with handsome flower spikes, and a tendency to colonize unless seedlings are kept in check.

The elder is guardian of all herbs according to folklore, and planting one of these will provide you with a green dye from the leaves and, from the berries, lilac (using alum mordant) or purple (using chrome).

SELECTED PLANTS FOR A DYE GARDEN

Part of the creative adventure of dyeing with plants is that the shades obtained can be varied considerably by using different mordants, so that madder, for example, can produce anything from light pink to dark brown.

- reds, pinks: bloodroot, chenopodium, madder, pokeberry, rose hips, sorrel
- yellows and orange: beetroot, coreopsis, dahlias, golden rod, heather, marigolds, Osage orange, pear leaves, rudbeckia, saffron, turmeric, weld, zinnias
- black: meadowsweet, walnut
- blues: blackberries, blueberries, dandelion root, elderberries, indigo, juniper berries, woad, yellow flag

- greens: bracken, dock, lily of the valley, nettles, weld
- browns: gipsywort, madder, sassafras, sumac, various barks (apple, birch, walnut), willow

Choosing Sites for Herbs

Choosing a suitable site for a herb needs preliminary assessment of factors such as the type of plant, the soil, the aspect, the exposure and the local temperature range. There are also practical considerations of space and appearance in relation to the rest of the garden. All this needs careful thought before starting to plant up sites.

Thymus vulgaris

Every form of gardening is artificial and depends for its success on matching as far as possible the natural environment of the plants. Herbs that you intend cultivating will be assembled in one place, and yet they come originally from all parts of the world and every kind of soil and climate.

Always find out where your herbs normally grow in the wild – it might be a sun-baked rocky hillside near the Mediterranean Sea or a well-watered rainforest where frost is unknown, a cool temperate woodland, or cold exposed cliff where wind keeps growth short and compact. Try to identify the warmest sheltered parts of the garden, the areas with the best drainage or dappled shade, corners where frost lingers or the sun arrives first in the morning, and allocate herbs according to their preferences. If you are planning a separate herb garden, assess its position at all times of the year and from all cultural aspects, and then choose the plants

Below: *A general mixed bed of herbs, combining, for example, borage, comfrey, lovage and lavender: this looks very effective against a backdrop of traditional wattle fencing.*

PLANNING A SMALL BORDER

Herbs for the back layer – 3 ft upwards
• *perennials: angelica, artemisia, bergamot, elecampane, fennel, liquorice, lovage, meadowsweet, rosemary, sea holly, shrub roses, European or American sweet cicely*
• *annuals and biennials: alexanders, foxglove, mullein*

Herbs for the middle section – 1 ft 6 in-3 ft
• *perennials: agrimony, balm, chicory, comfrey, costmary, curry plant, lavender, rampion, rue, sage, santolina, southernwood, St John's wort, tansy, tarragon, valerian, white horehound*
• *annuals and biennials: borage, bugloss, caraway, dill*

Herbs for the front edge – up to 1 ft 6 in
• *perennials: bistort, calamint, catmint, chamomile, chives, herb bennet, hyssop, lady's smock, marjoram, mint, sedum, sorrel, thyme, winter savory, wormwood, yarrow*
• *annuals and biennials: anise, basil, chervil, clary, coriander, cumin, marigold, parsley, summer savory*

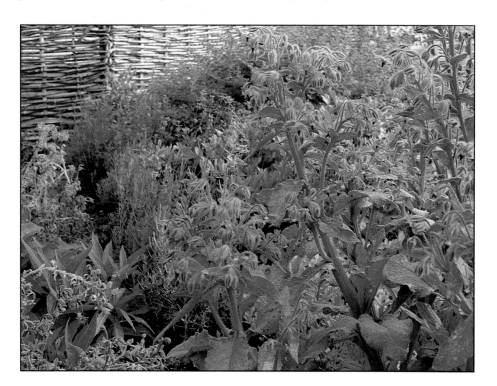

that are most likely to succeed in its various beds.

Remember that the term 'herbs' is used as a broad and imprecise classification, and includes plants with very different life cycles. Annuals and biennials are short-term plants, the former completing their growth from germination to shedding seed within a single season (some such as chervil can manage more than one generation per year). This partly determines where they are grown, for they will change rapidly in appearance and leave gaps in a planting scheme when they have died down. Biennials germinate and make leafy growth during their first season, survive the winter on the stored nutrients in their roots, and then flower and set seed the following year; if they are grown for their foliage, you can treat them as annuals, but for flower and seed crops they will need space for two years.

Perennials, which may be hardy or tender according to their origin, provide the framework of any herb garden design, for they are permanent and maintain continuity from one year to the next.

Size varies widely, with some herbs low-growing but liable to expand sideways into broad ground-hugging mats of foliage, while others are tall and dominating. Ultimate height and spread should always be taken into account when planning beds and herb gardens, together with a plant's tolerance of pruning and clipping, for many bulky subjects such as evergreen shrubs can be cut back to manageable size. Site plants of various heights according to their probable impact on an overall design: the tallest species work best in the center of island beds viewed from all sides or at the back of borders, with the shortest plants at the

PLANTING A HEDGE

1 Mark out and excavate a shallow trench running the length of the proposed hedge, and thoroughly fork over the soil in the bottom to ensure good drainage.

2 Hedging plants need plenty of nourishment in their early years, so add a generous amount of garden compost to the trench and lightly fork in.

3 Mark the center line of the hedge with string and pegs, and space out the plants, using a length of cane or wooden batten to measure equal distances between them.

4 Planted, firmed and watered in the refilled trench, the hedge will soon begin to fill out, ready for its first trim to shape.

front, although positioning a large, attractive specimen where it is least expected (within a sea of contrasting short plants, perhaps, or on a bend in a path to conceal an alcove) can produce a satisfying impact.

Growing herbs in containers is the ideal solution where considerations of space, soil or climate suggest a plant might be difficult to grow. This is not a poor substitute for open-ground cultivation, but an attractive branch of gardening in its own right. Most herbs

adapt to pots and other containers, and when well tended can create satisfying collections to enhance otherwise barren areas of the garden – courtyards, flights of steps, entrances and exits, for example – and make herb growing a practical choice for window boxes, balconies and roof gardens. It is easy to supply container-grown plants with the kind of soil they prefer, and to move them under cover or to sunny spots if they are sensitive to cold or exposure.

Above: *Raised beds built within stone walls are convenient sites for herbs such as rosemary. They offer good drainage and ease of picking.*

Above: *Shady woodland spots suit many herbs which do not tolerate direct sun and dry soil. Herbs such as peppermint may provide useful ground cover for barer patches beneath trees in cultivated gardens.*

Planning the Herb Garden

Formal or relaxed, utilitarian or decorative, a herb garden must be satisfying to look at and work in, and manageable in terms of your time, needs, energy and commitment. A complex parterre, for example, must be kept clipped, weed-free and carefully aligned for success, whereas the cottage garden approach of profusion without confusion may be more appropriate if you want plentiful supplies of useful herbs combined with cheerful diversity and low maintenance.

Levisticum officinale

Once you have explored the potential site and the chances of your chosen herbs liking the position, there is style to consider. This is an intangible but important matter, taking into account not only your personal tastes but the nature of the site, for any garden or border is intimately bonded to the house, and to the immediate and distant surroundings.

With a fairly clear vision of the garden you would like, you can draw together all the various elements in a final design. Measure the garden or plot, and mark its outline on graph

Above: *Design herb beds and borders to take advantage of contrasts between colors and shapes, but remember to match for height and impact.*

paper, together with existing assets such as shrubs and paths that are to be retained, and important nearby features – fences or hedges, large trees that might cast shade, and the house itself. Mark in with symbols the essential bones of the scheme, the new paths and beds, large plants, watercourses. The smaller the intended garden, the easier this planning stage will be, and for a simple bed of culinary herbs you might be able to omit drawing up a design altogether.

For larger plans always beware the illusion that you have more room in the garden than actually exists: it is easy on paper to draw a path or pack a large number of herbs into a given space, and then find that the result is hopelessly cramped or out of scale, or has unexpected visual effects on the rest of the garden. Look up the likely spread of trees and shrubs, mark this precisely on the plan, and then check frequently with the site itself; if necessary position stakes where significant plants and features are to go, or lay a garden hose on the ground to assess

Left: *Avoid mistakes and disappointment by making careful preliminary plans, drawing out the proposed design to scale to check its impact and feasibility.*

LAYING A PATH

1 Mark out and excavate the path, arranging stout boards along the sides with their upper edges at the finished surface level. Spread and compact a foundation of hardcore such as stones or broken brick.

2 Cover the base with a bed of sand, lightly tamped with the head of a rake to fill any gaps in the hardcore, and then rake a loose level surface in which to bed the bricks.

3 Arrange the bricks on the widest side in an attractive bond or pattern, firming them into place with the handle of a hammer and checking the surface in all directions with a spirit level as you go.

4 With all the bricks set out, spread more sand over the surface and brush repeatedly to fill all the joints; clear away any surplus sand.

5 Ease sand from the joints with a knife to create pockets for prostrate herbs which may be sown directly or, as here, planted as divisions from established specimens.

6 Tuck a little compost around the plants, firm into place and water if necessary; they will soon spread into mats and cushions of fragrant foliage.

the shape and course of a path or bed.

Work out planting schemes for individual beds and borders on separate sheets of paper only when you are satisfied with all this preliminary work make any necessary basic adjustments after trying out possible variations on the ground.

In addition to pictorial plans, you should also draw up a schedule of the work involved, because the various tasks are often best done in a particular order, perhaps at certain times of the year to ensure the least amount of disorder, mess and delay. Planting itself is almost the final operation and best timed for autumn in mild areas, or spring where winters are severe.

Before then you will need to repair or renovate existing hard structures such as paths, fences and walls, prune or move plants at the appropriate season, and remove turf or weeds to leave a clear site for marking out. Separate smaller beds can be prepared and planted piecemeal, but when planning a complete herb garden it is best to complete all these preliminary stages before transferring your design to the ground, using pegs driven in securely and joined with strings to mark the basic outlines. You can then dig over beds and borders to a suitable depth and condition, and set about constructing paths and hard edges.

Plant Requirements

Consideration should be given to the requirements of individual herbs for successful growth and yield; different surroundings are suitable for different herbs and a little time spent researching the ideal environment will help to produce a wonderful crop of pungent and decorative plants.

Lavandula spica

Although most of the well-known herbs are of Mediterranean origin and therefore prefer a sunny, free-draining position, re-creating the ecology they evolved in does not mean aiming deliberately for impoverished conditions. Only the nasturtium is recommended for hungry sites, because these encourage the production of flowers that might otherwise be usurped by lush leaf growth; but the result of improved flowering in the case of the nasturtium is often early death. It is worth remembering that most plants grown in gardens are often superior in form, size and performance to their relatives in the wild: the fact that they have adapted naturally to spartan surroundings is no reason to deny them care and nourishment.

It is fair to say, though, that aromatic herbs grown for flavoring or medicinal use are best grown in full sun, whereas those grown as pot herbs and leaf crops prefer moister conditions and some shelter from hot sunshine if they are to make plenty of growth. Arrange beds or the distribution of plants within a herb garden according to these needs, assembling leafy plants, for example, at the shady end of a border, in the shadow of shrubs, near hedges or beneath the canopy of open-pruned trees to provide them with a little dappled shade. Remember that variegated plants yield their best colors when exposed to morning and evening sunlight with a little shade at midday.

Similarly, free drainage is important for plants that are intolerant of damp conditions. These include plants with silver and grey foliage, which is usually produced by dense fine leaf hairs intended to trap moisture, developed as an adaptation to very dry conditions. Other plants of dubious hardiness may also succumb to prolonged damp around the stems. Raised beds or gravel mulches around stem bases can sometimes improve their chances of survival. Most woody-stemmed perennials need plenty of warm sunlight to ripen their growth and ensure

DIVIDING A BED

1 Segregate herbs with underground runners from other, more vulnerable plants with wide slates or pieces of durable panelling inserted vertically.

2 Replace the soil on both sides of the division, and firm into place with your heel or the handle of a trowel.

3 An invasive herb such as mint can then be planted a little distance from the inconspicuous division.

that they are well prepared to withstand winter temperatures.

Herbs that like damp, partially shaded sites, on the other hand, only thrive where their needs are met, both hot dry soil and gloomy waterlogged positions proving intolerable to them. Herbaceous perennial herbs, in particular, need to make maximum growth during the growing season to stock their roots with enough nutrients for survival and re-emergence the following spring.

Most herbs need shelter of some kind from the extremes of wind and frost. Though they might survive in the wild, their growth is often stunted by wind-pruning and frost injury, and you will do them a favor by enclosing beds and borders with windbreak hedges or fences that reduce their exposure. You will reap the benefits in summer, when the still sheltered air is heavy with the concentrated fragrance of volatile oils. Make sure, however, that the garden is not so enclosed that it becomes a frost pocket, without gateways or openings for cold air to drain away from susceptible plants.

SLOPING GROUND

Level ground is not essential unless you are planning an impressive parterre or knot garden, which really needs construction on a prepared platform in the same way as a bowling green or formal lawn. For most other herb schemes sloping ground, especially a dry bank, is ideal as a means of guaranteeing good drainage and, if it faces the sun for a large part of the day, plenty of warmth and light. There are enough prostrate and trailing herb varieties to ensure adequate ground cover and protection against soil erosion on a bank, but for larger specimens or where the incline is very steep,

making simple terraces or small level planting pockets will help with rapid establishment and any watering needed until plants are self-reliant. Paths can be cut as a series of steps, their outline perhaps softened by cascading thymes, ground-hugging Corsican mint, or tufts of chamomile and the creeping savory *Satureja spicigera*.

Above: *Herbs that need warm conditions do well when planted along the base of a brick wall facing the sun, which remains warm even after nightfall.*

Right: *A simple pit surrounded with firm walls of bricks or old wooden beams provides a useful bed for larger herbs, or (as here) a propagation and nursery frame that can be covered in cold weather.*

Above: *Stepping stones made from sawn log sections or paving slabs are a simple means of providing access for planting and maintenance in larger beds, and soon merge with the herbs as these grow and spread.*

HERBS FOR HEAVY SOILS

Although wet clays and other intractable soils will always benefit from some improvement to open their texture and speed drainage, the following herbs can usually cope well, especially if the surface is mulched in summer to prevent drought and cracking. Sunny or shaded sites are suitable, except where stated otherwise.

• alexanders	• angelica
• borage (sun)	• calendula
• chives (sun)	• comfrey
• fennel (sun)	• lemon balm (sun)
• lovage	• mint
• nasturtium (sun)	• sage
• sorrel	• sweet cicely

Structuring the Herb Garden

The design of a formal herb garden, whether it is a complex of knots or a simple wheel with radiating spokes dividing beds of culinary plants, allows plenty of scope for imagination. As William Lawson wrote in the seventeenth century, 'For special forms in squares, there are as many as there are devices in Gardeners' brains.' Simplicity is essential, for an elaborate layout will merely look confused once plants start to grow, and will only be comprehensible if viewed from above.

Gratiola officinalis

Graph paper is essential, as are accurate measurements. Sketch in the outlines of beds and borders as a rough guide, by all means, but decide first on the layout and dimensions of paths. Ornament is one thing, access at all seasons for harvesting and tending plants another, and all paths should be wide enough for comfortable passage (especially between shrubs after heavy rain) and must reach all parts of the garden. Main paths should be at least 2 ft wide, more if you use a wheelbarrow or need wheelchair access. You can make subsidiary paths narrower – 12 in might be enough – or you could use stepping stones instead of a continuous surface. Position the odd slab in large beds to stand on, or limit the beds' width to about 4 ft so that all herbs are within arm's reach.

While balance and good proportion are important in planning the layout of beds, there is no reason why an irregular herb garden cannot be as successful as a classically symmetrical one. Draw out several geometrical patterns of beds on tracing paper laid over the garden outline drawn to scale on squared paper, and check their measurements for practicality. Leave room for seats, statuary and other features, and remember that hedges occupy substantial space – allow a 12 in width for dwarf hedges, more for taller ones.

A series of small beds, each planted with a single type of herb, provides simple bold blocks of color and texture, but more comprehensive plant collections need larger beds, perhaps organized according to color, height or use. With elaborate designs, always measure the diagonals to make sure they are truly symmetrical, and take all measurements accurately, starting where possible from a base line – that is, the longest straight line that can be measured on the site – which can be used as a reference for all other

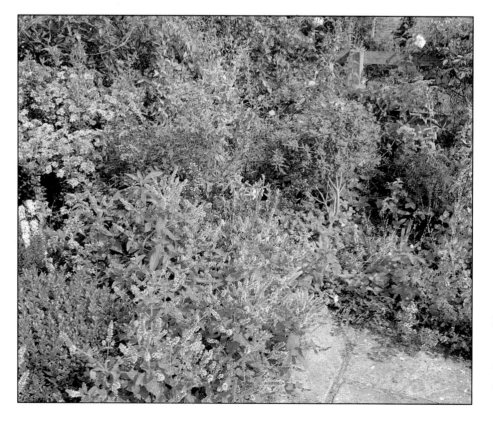

Left: *Herbs adapt to a number of styles and designs, not least to a relaxed cottage garden arrangement where the plants can grow and flower with their natural informality.*

HERB SPIRAL

1 Arrange bricks in a gradually increasing number of courses to create the outline of a spiral bed.

2 Spread a drainage layer of pea-sized gravel on the surface of lower levels, omitting areas where moisture-loving herbs are to grow.

3 Add garden compost to part of the lower level for hungry herbs such as parsley, basil and leaf coriander.

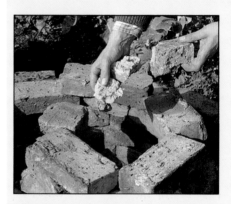

4 Partly fill the upper levels with broken bricks and rubble to ensure good drainage for herbs that like dry soil.

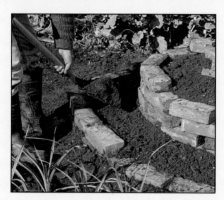

5 Fill between the parallel walls with good topsoil, and tamp into place or leave to settle.

6 Arrange the herbs for dry soil near the top and moisture- and nutrient-loving species at the base.

distances. Leave a string marking this line in position if possible to allow easy transfer of the design from paper to ground.

RAISED BEDS

Early herb gardens comprised a series of beds, laid out as functional squares and rectangles or in decorative shapes; these were raised slightly above the level of intervening paths with the soil held in place by edging boards. Raised beds have several advantages over ground-level cultivation: their layout establishes a strong design pattern, and it is easier to improve individual beds than to change the nature of the soil on a large scale, and less bending is involved in cultivating the plants. A single layer of thick wooden planks or edging boards, or two or three courses of bricks, will considerably increase the rooting depth where soils are shallow, while the sides of beds can be raised as high as necessary for the comfort of disabled and elderly gardeners. Higher sides, though, may need foundations and footings for stability, together with a series of holes for drainage.

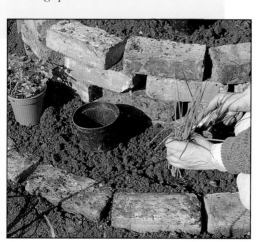

7 Finally, plant out the herbs and water thoroughly.

Preparing the Site

Many plants are site-specific, only growing well where conditions are perfect. Fortunately the commonest herbs tolerate a wide range of soils, although their performance may be less than ideal – silver and gray herbs, for example, thrive in light, sandy ground, but in the same place sage and winter savory soon develop bare stems and need frequent propagation, and leafy annual herbs quickly bolt to seed in a dry season.

Teucrium chamaedrys

Recreating a plant's preferred habitat is the ideal way to ensure success. Most of us, however, have to compromise by making the most of our garden soil. For positive health plants need enough moisture to maintain growth but not so much that their roots decay in airless surroundings; a balanced supply of nutrients and minerals in a soil that is not too acid or alkaline; sufficient warmth to sustain active growth, and freedom from weed competition. Any soil improvement must take all these factors into account.

Sandy soil is easy to work and warms up quickly, but soluble nutrients are easily leached out by rain, and drought may seriously check the growth of all but the toughest Mediterranean species. Adding plenty of garden compost before planting, together with annual mulches and occasional supplementary feeding to restore depleted fertility, helps to fortify the soil without destroying its naturally free drainage.

The tiny particles of clay readily stick together, producing wet, airless soil that sets hard and cracks in dry weather. Heavy ground with a large proportion of clay is potentially very fertile if you can improve its texture by digging in grit, coarse sand, leaf litter and bulky manure or compost to help aeration. A permanent mulch will protect the surface from being compacted by heavy rainfall and from drying out in hot sunshine.

Pools of water lingering on the surface of heavy waterlogged soils usually indicate poor drainage. Digging can relieve the problem if this is due to surface compaction, while deeper cultivation will break up a hard 'pan' – an impervious layer some distance below the surface. If saturation recurs, you may have to install a system of drainage pipes for permanent improvement unless you confine your herb collection to marshy species.

BEDS FOR WET GROUND

An alternative treatment for wet ground is to increase the depth of free-draining topsoil available for plants by creating raised beds. These are equally effective for coping with

HERBS FOR LIGHT, SANDY SOIL

Many herbs tolerate light, dry soils, but these are particularly suitable. Winter rain may remove large amounts of lime and nutrients each year, so be prepared to feed or compost the soil annually.

- alkanet
- arnica
- broom
- chervil
- coriander
- dianthus
- fennel
- hound's tongue
- lavender
- lemon verbena
- marjoram
- artemisia
- savory
- tarragon
- wormwood

- anise
- borage
- centaury
- chives
- cumin
- evening primrose
- foxglove
- hyssop
- lemon balm
- alfalfa
- sweet clover
- rosemary
- southernwood
- thyme

soils that are shallow, or too acid or alkaline to suit most species. Raised beds are not a modern innovation, but date back to medieval gardens. They may be enclosed by low walls of bricks, stone or timber boarding and their width is best limited to about 4 ft so that you can reach the center without walking on the soil.

Dig over the enclosed area thoroughly, work in as much organic material as you can to improve texture and drainage, and add 6 in of topsoil, perhaps saved from the making of paths, or bought. Finally cover the surface with an organic mulch that can be stirred in annually with a fork to maintain fertility.

CLEARING GROUND

The site for a herb garden is best prepared in autumn. Start by eliminating weeds, especially invasive perennial kinds that will be difficult to remove after planting; these can be forked out carefully or cleared with one or two applications of systemic weedkiller. If the area is under grass, skim this off

HERBS FOR CHALKY SOIL

- calamint
- chickweed
- cowslip
- elder
- juniper
- lemon balm
- lungwort
- mignonette
- Pasque flower
- rosemary
- sage
- Solomon's seal
- wormwood

- centaury
- chicory
- dianthus
- hound's tongue
- lavender
- lily of the valley
- marjoram
- mullein
- periwinkle
- roses
- salad burnet
- thyme
- yarrow

with a spade, stack neatly and cover with black plastic sheet until it decays into fibrous loam for potting.

Correct any drainage problems and dig the bed thoroughly. Dress with lime if the soil is too acid, and leave the surface rough over winter to be broken down by frost. In early spring treat any weeds that have appeared, and then fork in a good dressing of compost or decayed manure. Rake the

surface level, and leave the ground for a few weeks to settle before marking out the design.

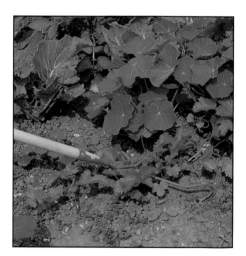

Above: *A hand cultivator with prongs can be useful for clearing the site of weeds.*

COMFREY COMPOST

1 Recycling vigorous perennials such as comfrey returns precious minerals and nutrients to the soil. Cut the larger foliage, leaving the youngest leaves to provide further crops later.

2 Soak the leaves in water to make a liquid feed, or add them to the compost heap as this is built; there they will decompose and release their goodness.

Healthy Herbs

Mentha piperita

A good collection of herbs is an enduring asset and healthy herbs are essential for a functioning garden of plants. Sensible planting arrangements, soil types and the availability of light are all important considerations when beginning a new herb bed or renovating an existing one.

A herb garden is an enduring asset, so do not be over-hasty in getting started. With the site prepared, construct any edgings and paths, except for gravel which is best laid after planting to avoid depositing soil on it.

Although container-grown herbs can be planted at almost any time of the year, autumn is the perfect season (especially for bare-root plants) unless winters are very cold or the soil heavy, in which case wait until mid-spring. If you have to wait several months before planting, use the bed for a display of annual flowers or grow a 'green manure' crop of mustard, clover or vetch to dig in later as a soil improver.

Try to fill a whole bed at once, even if this means assembling a collection of herbs over a period of time. They can be kept in their containers, or transferred temporarily to a nursery bed where you might be able to take cuttings or divisions to supplement your stock. Bare-root plants must be heeled in to a piece of spare ground if they are not to be planted immediately.

Be generous with quantities; trees, shrubs and invasive herbs can be planted singly, but others, particularly small edging plants, are best ordered in quantity for an instant impression of lush establishment. Always choose young, short-jointed bushy plants with

PEST AND DISEASE CONTROL

Treating your herbs well by watering, feeding or propagating whenever necessary helps to maintain their vigor and so avoid disorders that normally affect ailing plants.

Any problems that do occur should be treated promptly. Aphids are perhaps the most common pests, and may be controlled by spraying with derris, or rotenone, which is harmless to their natural predators. Quassia is effective against caterpillars if there are too many to pick off by hand. Slugs and snails are also best controlled by picking off.

Diseases are occasionally more serious, especially fungal disorders such as rust, which commonly affects mint, as well as violets and other subjects. Cut down rusted growth to ground level for burning, and scorch the crown and surrounding soil with a flame gun; if all else fails use a commercial fungicide or alternatively transfer clean-rooted divisions to fresh soil.

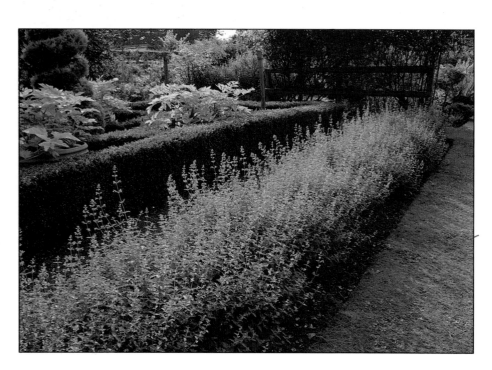

Left: *Some herbs are attractive enough to mass on their own. The many forms of thyme are favourites for planting as hedges, edgings and flowering borders.*

Right: *A healthy purple sage plant. For their strongest color such plants need full sunlight, though even in light shade the young tips will display their characteristic leaf colors.*

PLASTIC MULCHES

If you suspect the ground is still full of weed seeds or root fragments, or if the soil is very light and liable to dry out quickly, you can use a plastic mulch to suppress weed growth and retain moisture. Prepare the soil in the usual way when it is moist and rake the surface level, removing as many stones as possible. Spread a sheet of heavy-duty black plastic sheet or woven matting across the bed, and secure the edges by wedging them in the soil. Cut holes or crosses in the sheet through which to plant the herbs, and then cover the whole surface with a layer of gravel, or shredded bark or cocoa shells.

INVASIVE HERBS

Herbs such as mint, tarragon and woodruff are irrepressible colonizers, their creeping roots eventually taking over large areas of ground and infiltrating neighbouring plants. Restrain their invasiveness by planting them in containers, either above ground or buried in the soil. Large pots, bottomless buckets or thick plastic bags perforated with drainage holes are ideal. They can be filled with good garden soil, or a soil and compost mixture, which will sustain them for two or three years before the contents need division and replanting in fresh soil.

a good, healthy color, and make sure they are fully hardened off if bought in spring.

PLANTING

Choose a pleasant day for planting, and one on which you have the time to finish an area completely. Water plants well, whether they are in pots or the open ground, and then arrange them on the surface according to your ground plan – but mark the positions for bare-root plants with stakes or labels, rather than expose them to drying out. Check the overall effect and make sure everything has room to develop, although to avoid unsightly gaps you might prefer to space certain plants more densely and then sacrifice some later as others demand room.

Plant edgings first, together with strategic plants such as trees, shrubs or anything with a large rootball – stake these where necessary, and tread the soil firm around larger plants. Spread out the roots of bare-root specimens, working soil between them as you refill the hole, and make sure the finished surface matches the soil mark on their stems. Re-level the intervening soil before planting the other herbs. Prune growing tips and side shoots of shrubby plants to encourage bushy growth. Label everything clearly, and then water the whole bed to settle the soil around the roots.

Looking after the Herb Garden

Herbs are relatively free from serious disorders, especially if you start with healthy plants in the first place. However, every plant depends for its welfare on the condition of the soil in which it grows, and the annual management routine in a herb garden should concentrate on building up and maintaining the soil's nutrients and vitality.

*Origanum
marjoranum*

WATERING AND FEEDING

Soils lose water through drainage or evaporation at different rates according to their type and condition: clay, for example, retains moisture for much longer than sandy soil, which in a hot dry season may need thorough watering at least every week. Plants can only absorb food in solution, so maintaining adequate moisture at the roots is essential for uninterrupted growth. The best way to ensure this is to add manure or compost to the soil to increase its content of humus, partly decomposed organic material that soaks up water like a sponge and releases it slowly, together with essential nutrients.

If the soil has been enriched with compost or decayed manure during initial preparations, it should be sufficient to spread a layer of compost annually over the surface of the moist soil in spring to maintain humus levels. Most aromatic herbs will then flourish without supplementary watering. Indeed, try not to be too generous when watering: too much water can dilute the essential oils, and may injure herbs that prefer relatively dry conditions.

Leafy herbs will need watering in a dry season to keep the soil constantly moist, while plants grown for their fruits or pods benefit most if watered when in flower and again while their crops are swelling. If you do water, soak plants thoroughly, and spread a further mulch afterwards to prevent evaporation. Plants in containers need regular watering, as will recently introduced herbs, especially if planted in summer. Be prepared to water new trees in dry weather for at least a season after planting.

As long as the soil is mulched annually with a light dressing of compost, most herbs will thrive without supplementary feeding. Too rich a soil, in fact, encourages soft rank growth with less flavor and perfume. Plants grown as bulky leaf crops sometimes benefit from an application of dried blood to supply extra nitrogen after a wet winter on light soils, and fruit quality is improved by a spring dressing of general fertilizer such as seaweed meal or blood, fish and bone. Avoid using artificial fertilizers, which may unbalance soil conditions and reduce the herbs' concentration of essential soils and active substances.

MULCHING

An essential part of soil care and plant health, mulching involves covering the

DIVIDING COMFREY

1 Vigorous clump-forming herbs such as bergamot, lovage and comfrey need dividing every few years to keep plants young and robust. Dig whole clumps for splitting, or use a spade to slice off outer portions from growing plants.

2 With a very sharp knife, cut these cleanly into small segments, each with a tuft of leaves or a dormant bud, and plenty of healthy roots. Replant immediately in good soil.

MAKING COMPOST

Apart from being a useful soil improver in the early stages of making a herb garden, animal manure is too rich for feeding all but the greediest plants. It can be used, however, as just one of the ingredients in a compost heap, where it will blend with plant waste to produce the ideal material for mulching and soil improvement. Site the compost heap on bare soil in a wire enclosure or commercial container, starting with a layer of plant stems and coarse material to let air penetrate the heap. Build the heap in layers, mixing organic household waste, manure, lawn mowings, weeds and discarded plants; avoid seeding and diseased plants, and pass any woody stems through a shredder first. Parts of herbs are particularly suitable ingredients, especially nettles, comfrey and yarrow, which all help the compost to ferment. Between the layers spread a thin dressing of garden lime, or gypsum if you do not want to increase the alkalinity of your soil. Cover the completed heap with plastic sheeting or old carpets. Leave it for a few months, then turn the contents to ensure even decomposition.

ground to protect it from erosion, rapid drying and structural deterioration after heavy rain or hot sun, and also to smother weeds.

An organic mulch of compost, pulverized bark or cocoa shells can be used for plants that like moist conditions, but herbs from hot dry habitats are better mulched with an inorganic material such as gravel or grit to prevent their stems from rotting – this is especially important on heavy soils that may remain wet for a large part of the year. Always spread a mulch when the soil is moist, and keep the material away from woody plant stems to ensure free drainage.

WEEDING

Although plants normally prefer to live in communities rather than alone, common weeds compete too energetically to allow them to grow

Above: *Herbs in constant use, as in this collection of culinary plants, need routine care if they are to prosper and stay in good condition: pruning or cutting back, watering, feeding and regular propagation all help maintain continuity.*

unchecked. A permanent mulch will suppress most annual weeds, which should otherwise be hoed or pulled by hand while still small. Perennial weeds such as buttercup, thistle and ground elder or goutweed are more tenacious and may be a problem even where the soil is mulched. Fork or pull them up with as much root as possible, or paint them individually with systemic weed-killer. Check when weeding, though, that you are not pulling up a potentially useful plant. Many herbs seed themselves and their seedlings can be transplanted to a nursery bed for growing on, while many weeds have

Left: *Cold frames can be a useful extension to beds and greenhouses, providing extra space and protection in the colder weather.*

Below: *Terracotta blanching pots can be placed over certain herbs to encourage early growth.*

medicinal or culinary uses and so may be worth leaving or growing elsewhere.

The appearance and qualities of herbs change as the season progresses, but light pruning checks this by redirecting energy into new growth, keeping plants in good condition for longer. Dead-heading borage, pot marigolds and other annuals will prevent their setting seed and so prolong flowering for a few more weeks. This is also a useful precaution with prolific seed producers such as fennel and angelica, whose deep-rooted seedlings can take over a herb border – but leave a few heads to mature if you do need more seeds. Self-seeding may be a virtue, of course: you can have continuous supplies of chervil if this short-lived annual is left to seed itself in a permanent bed, while in its second year a parsley plant will sow a patch of seedlings for transplanting elsewhere.

Perennials grown for the soft tips of their shoots are best cut back once or twice as their stems start to age: mint and lemon balm, for example, will produce further flushes of young growth if pruned to ground level before their shoots reach full height. Shrubby perennials are best clipped lightly after flowering to keep the plants tidy and stimulate new side shoots, but if grown formally they will need more frequent trimming. Hedges of santolina, hyssop, rosemary and germander should be clipped in early summer and again two or three months later, and may be pruned hard in spring if they have grown too large.

AUTUMN CARE

As frost threatens, tender herbs such as basil, lemon verbena and scented pelargoniums should be dug up for potting and growing on indoors. Take cuttings from any of doubtful hardiness, or transplant a specimen to the cold frame as insurance against loss. Either leave dead stems on herbaceous perennials over winter to provide a little insulation against frost and wind, or cut them down for composting and insulate the crowns of cold-sensitive plants with a covering of bracken, leaves or straw held in place with wire netting. Remember that different varieties of the same herb may vary in hardiness, so check their individual needs. Always clear away fallen

FRESH CULINARY HERBS AVAILABLE IN WINTER

- burnet – outdoors or under cloches
- chives – under cloches or indoors in pots
- mint – in a cold frame or in large pots and boxes indoors
- rosemary – outdoors or in pots

- winter savory – outdoors or in pots indoors
- chervil – outdoors, in a cold frame or indoors in pots
- marjoram – outdoors or in pots indoors
- pelargoniums – indoors in pots
- sage – outdoors

leaves from prostrate herbs that might otherwise rot beneath them.

THE HERB GARDEN IN WINTER

With herbaceous plants now dormant, interest will focus on evergreen species. Not all these can withstand a bleak winter, so check their hardiness and if necessary arrange windbreaks of sacking or plastic mesh to filter cold winds. Shake off settled snow before its weight damages branches.

EXTENDING THE SEASON

To ensure a supply of basic herbs during winter, use some form of protection to keep them in active growth. Cloches and small covers set over parsley, chives and mint in autumn will prolong their usefulness for several extra weeks, or you can transfer a few plants to a cold frame where they will be available all winter if the frame is covered with matting in hard frost. Lettuce, coriander and chervil can be sown in cold frames to crop in winter. Many other herbs such as thyme, tarragon and sage may be dug up and potted for use indoors, with a few pots kept in reserve in a frame or greenhouse to take their place when they are exhausted. Some herbs respond to forcing, especially mint, whose roots can be dug up in late winter and buried in boxes of potting compost to make early growth in the greenhouse. Out of doors, cloches placed over dormant plants will revive them a little earlier than normal, while crops such as rhubarb, seakale and Good King Henry are usually forced into growth by covering them with boxes or blanching pots.

Right: *A sheltered area or potting shed is ideal for transplanting herbs and storing equipment.*

USING A COLD FRAME

1 A cold frame is a valuable accessory, both for growing plants out of season and for housing cuttings and young plants, such as these thyme seedlings, in their early stages.

2 Adequate humidity and protection from low temperatures or bright sunlight are essential, so cover the frame when necessary, but remember to admit ventilation whenever possible.

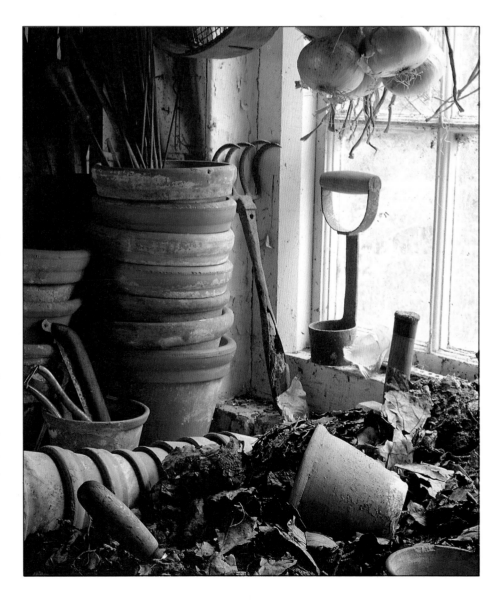

Propagating Herbs

Seasoned professionals and amateur gardeners alike get immense satisfaction from raising new plants. Your collection may start with a few bought herbs in pots, but sooner or later you will probably want to grow your own from seed or by rooting live parts of a plant. Some herbs can be started in more than one way while others need a particular technique; whichever method is used, remember always to start with healthy material or seeds from a reputable source to avoid disappointment.

Anagallis arvensis

GROWING FROM SEED

Most herb species can be raised from seed, although this method takes the longest to produce a mature plant and is not recommended for named cultivars, especially variegated kinds, as seedlings do not always resemble the parent plant. Seed sowing is the quickest way to grow a particular plant in large quantities, and the usual method of raising annual and biennial herbs, wild flowers, salad and vegetable herbs, species from other countries and easily germinated perennials such as chives, fennel, feverfew, lovage, rue, salad burnet, European and American sweet cicely and winter savory.

Although a seed is a potential plant just waiting to grow, it will only germinate when conditions are right. For most, a combination of adequate warmth, moisture and air is enough to trigger them into life, but others have special requirements which depend on the kind of surroundings they normally meet in the wild.

The seeds of juniper, woodruff, European sweet cicely and violets, for example, are protected by a hard, resistant coat against early germination when temperatures are too cold, and they depend on frost to break this down – a process called stratification.

SOWING

1 Fill a sterilized tray with a moist seed growing medium. Level and firm lightly if this is soil-based; simply tap the tray to settle soil-less composts.

2 Scatter small seeds evenly and thinly over the whole surface of the compost; larger seeds can be spaced at regular intervals.

3 Some seeds need light for germination, but others prefer darkness and must be covered with compost that has been sifted to remove any lumps or debris.

4 Sprinkle this fine compost evenly over the seeds to the recommended depth, label the tray and cover with plastic or glass to conserve moisture.

Sown in autumn, they may be left outdoors exposed to winter weather, or you can artificially break their dormancy by mixing the seeds with damp sand in a plastic bag, and leaving this in a refrigerator for about two months before sowing in warm conditions.

Hard-coated leguminous seeds need penetration by moisture before they will grow. This can be speeded up by scarification, a method that involves carefully nicking the coat with a sharp knife or gently thinning part of it with sandpaper; soaking overnight in warm water is an alternative way. Some ordinary seeds need light, others darkness, to trigger germination, so always follow the sowing instructions on seed packets carefully to make sure you have provided the right conditions.

SOWING OUTDOORS

The normal sowing time for the majority of plants is early to mid-spring, just as soon as the soil is warm enough to support active growth. Wait until new weed seedlings appear or the first hedgerow buds break as an indication of the best time.

Vegetables and herbs needed in quantity are sown in drills in the kitchen garden, others in shorter rows in a nursery bed; flowering herbs may be sown where they are to grow, either in short rows or in circular furrows made by pressing the rim of a pot into the soil surface. Wherever you are sowing, always fork, weed and rake the soil into a crumbly level seedbed first, and in cold weather warm the ground for a week or two beforehand by covering it with cloches.

Use a rake handle or garden stake to mark out a shallow depression in the soil for short drills, or draw the corner of the rake along a tight garden line for longer rows. Sow the

GROWING BASIL

1 Basil seeds may be sown individually in soil blocks to save pricking out later, or seedlings can be transferred from seed trays.

2 The richer compost mixture of the soil blocks combined with heat and regular watering encourage rapid early growth.

3 With two pairs of true leaves, these seedlings are well established and ready for potting up.

4 After hardening off, these young basil plants will soon be ready for transfer to the open garden.

seeds in the bottom of the drill, and then cover with a thin layer of soil and gently tamp with the back of the rake head to ensure good contact between soil and seeds. In very dry weather flood the open drill with water, allow to drain before sowing, and then cover with dry soil.

Keep the sown area well watered until seedlings appear. When large enough to handle these should be thinned to leave plants 2-4 in apart. Most annual herbs can be left to grow at this spacing, but biennials and perennials may need thinning again or transplanting to another patch of ground until large enough to be moved to their permanent positions.

SOWING UNDER GLASS

This is the best method of raising half-hardy annuals and early crops, together with those herbs that need extra warmth or pot cultivation, and any that are particularly precious or expensive.

Use seed trays, pots or shallow pans according to the quantity of seeds, first cleaning and sterilizing the containers with soapy water and a little ammonia or disinfectant. Cover the drainage holes of earthenware pots with a few broken shards before filling with a moist seed compost; plastic containers can be filled without a drainage layer. Tap the pot sharply to settle the contents or gently firm with a flat board, and then scatter the seeds thinly and evenly over the surface.

Dust a thin layer of compost over them, as deep as the diameter of the seeds – but any that need light for germination should be simply pressed gently into the surface. Label and seal the pot and cover it with a clear plastic bag, or with a piece of glass and a sheet of opaque paper where darkness is required.

Stand the containers in a warm place, and keep the soil moist during germination, either misting it when dry or standing the container in shallow water until moist patches appear on the surface. Check frequently to see if seedlings are emerging - germination may take only a few days, or several weeks or more for slow growers such as parsley and bay. Once the first shoots appear, remove the covering and move them into the light, but avoid bright sunlight until they are stronger.

MOUNDING

Evergreen perennials such as sage can quickly develop into impressive mounds of shrubby growth.

1 When old woody herbs develop bare lower stems, they can be propagated by mounding.

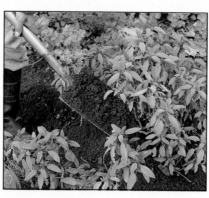

2 Clear out any dead stems and leaves, and then heap soil in the center of the bush.

3 Leave for a few months. Each of the branches will have rooted and can be detached as a new plant.

LAYERING ROSEMARY

1 Choose a low, flexible branch, remove some of the leaves where it touches the soil, and cut a shallow notch to induce rooting.

2 Scoop out a shallow depression for the prepared section of branch, and hold it in place with a wire loop or clothes pin.

3 Cover the wounded section and peg with good topsoil, and firm gently. In dry weather water the layer (but not the parent plant) to hasten rooting.

STRIKING CUTTINGS

1 Prepare a gritty, free-draining rooting mixture by blending sharp sand with an equal volume of peat, peat substitute or seed compost.

2 Trim the cuttings to size, using a very sharp knife to cut through the stem just below a node. Remove the lowest pair of leaves.

3 Fill a pot with the mixture and insert a cutting in each. Water in the cuttings and enclose in a plastic bag supported on short canes.

When seedlings are large enough (usually when they have made true leaves in addition to their seed leaves), they will need pricking out (transplanting singly) except in the case of large seeds sown individually in small pots and those to be planted out or potted on intact. Replant the seedlings up to the base of their seed leaves in separate pots of moist potting medium or about 2 in apart in seed trays.

DIVISION

Division is used to multiply herbs that form clumps of rooted stems, and also to rejuvenate older specimens where the centre of the clump has died out, leaving a ring of young material. The whole crown of the plant is eased from the soil with a fork, during winter dormancy or in early spring as growth revives. Divide it into segments by plunging two forks back to back into the mass of growth and forcing them apart; smaller crowns can be split with a sharp knife or by tearing off rooted portions. Replant divisions firmly in fresh soil at the same depth as the original crown.

LAYERING

Layering is a slow but foolproof method of inducing the stem of a woody perennial such as sage, lavender or honeysuckle to make roots of its own while it is still nourished by the parent plant.

MOUNDING

When whole plants are layered to root large numbers of cuttings, or to restore a neglected herb that has become bare at the base, the technique is known as mounding or stooling. It is very useful for salvaging unpruned lavender bushes, but can be used on any woody herb; it is also the standard way to multiply rootstocks for fruit trees.

CUTTINGS

Cuttings are small portions of stem or root, trimmed off and induced to grow roots of their own. There are three main kinds of stem cutting: hardwood, taken in autumn from woody stems of trees and shrubs and rooted outdoors or in a cold frame over winter; semi-hardwood, taken in mid- to late summer from side shoots with a ripe base and often a 'heel' of old wood; and softwood cuttings taken in spring or summer, using the soft tips of the current year's growth. The differences are largely technical and most plants can be propagated by more than one method; clipping shrubby herbs and hedges to shape often yields plenty of cutting material.

Always use sturdy, healthy nonflowering shoots about 3-4 in long; hardwood cuttings rooted in the ground should be two or three times this length. Trim carefully just below a leaf joint with a razor blade or sharp knife. Strip the leaves from the lower half of the cutting using a knife or by pulling them away to leave a clean wound. The base of the cuttings can be dipped in a hormone rooting preparation as an insurance before inserting them firmly in a well-drained cuttings compost. Strike soft cuttings in pots in sealed plastic bags or a propagator, others in a cold frame or outdoors in a sheltered place. Shade from bright sunlight, and pot on or transplant to a nursery bed as soon as the cuttings are growing well.

Potted Herb Gardens

Lack of available ground need not stop you from making a collection of herbs, for most adapt readily to cultivation in pots and other containers. Even if most of your herbs grow in the open garden, growing some of your favorite kinds in pots adds a further dimension to herb gardening.

Origanum vulgare

Pots can be arranged near the house in decorative groups for easy access, their mobility allowing you to move them around to follow the sun as the season progresses or to shelter them from cold winds. You can bring them indoors in winter to maintain supplies or even for guests to help themselves to herbs at the table. Larger tubs or troughs provide room for several kinds to grow together as permanent miniature herb gardens, positioned where they get all the sun or shade they might need. In gardens on poor ground, container growing is the best way of providing perfect soil.

Almost any kind of container is suitable and the range is infinite, from wooden boxes, clay pots and stone urns, to used growing bags and large paint tins, cattle troughs and coal scuttles. Any you choose must be large enough to house plants comfortably – aim for a minimum 8 in diameter and depth - and should have adequate free drainage at the base to shift surplus water and so avoid sour, stagnant conditions at the roots. Provide several drainage holes in the base, together with a few more in the sides just above the base if the containers are not supported off the ground by small blocks or pieces of tile to let water drain away.

Try to match containers to their intended plants. Terracotta is an attractive material sympathetic to more decorative herbs such as a collection of colored sages (golden 'Icterina', cream and pink 'Tricolor' and red 'Purpurescens', for example) or the many kinds of scented-leaved geraniums. A larger tub would suit an informal arrangement of rosemary, hyssop, thyme and golden marjoram, and if mounted on castors could be moved to a greenhouse or conservatory for winter use. Utilitarian containers such as bottomless buckets or 2 gallon paint containers may be hidden behind more ornamental pots to house taller invasive herbs such as tarragon, sorrel, horseradish, comfrey and mint. Used growing bags are ideal for annual and biennial herbs such as basil, chervil and parsley, or for growing out-of-season supplies of mint in the greenhouse. Wooden 'Versailles' pots and similar large formal containers are best reserved for specimen bay trees, herb topiary, or perhaps a trained quince planted with annual nasturtiums, lettuce and trailing New Zealand spinach at the base.

POTTING ON

1 As plants develop they need to be moved on to increasingly large containers. Free drainage is essential and depends on a preliminary layer of small stones or gravel.

2 The pot is then part-filled with the appropriate growing medium, the plant is tapped from its old pot and centered in the new one, and the remaining space is filled with soil.

1 Leafy bushes of bay are reliable in containers, but be sure to plant in pots of adequate size; one such as this will sustain growth for several years before it is too small.

2 While there is still room in the container, smaller herbs such as parsley, thyme and marjoram planted around the base will transform the pot into a miniature garden.

Above: *Evergreen bay (*Laurus nobilis*) is a popular container shrub for formal situations, as here where a pyramid-trained specimen stands sentinel in a painted 'Versailles' box.*

PLANTING

The easiest way to start any potted collection is to buy pots of young herbs from a specialist nurseryman, and plant these straight into new containers. Cutting the tips of shoots for use will keep them compact for several months before they need potting on or exchanging for smaller plants. A stouter herb such as rosemary, lavender or sage can be started by rooting several cuttings together in a small pot and then transferring them as a single plant to the container until they become too large and need replacement.

At planting time check that drainage holes are clear and then cover them with a layer of gravel, stones or a few shards from broken clay pots. Over this spread a thin layer of peat or a moisture-retentive peat substitute before filling the pot with a soil-based potting mixture. Soil-less growing media can be difficult to moisten once completely dry, and as most contain fertilizers that are soon exhausted, supplementary feeding is often necessary after only a few weeks. They are easier to handle and lighter than soil-based mixes, but this may be a disadvantage outdoors where weight confers stability. John Innes No 2 or Cornell mix is a good commercial mixture, or you can blend your own from 7 parts good garden soil, 3 parts peat or leafmould, 2 parts horticultural sand, and a little seaweed fertilizer – but watch out for possible weed seedlings.

POT CARE

Herbs in pots need special attention, as they are totally dependent on the gardener for their welfare. Their greatest need is water: the toughest drought-loving herb cannot survive for long in bone-dry soil and you must therefore check regularly (daily or even twice daily in a hot summer) that the soil stays consistently moist. Leafy herbs will appreciate an occasional feed of houseplant fertilizer, but for others annual re-potting or top-dressing is enough to replenish their diet.

Young herbs in small pots need to be transferred to larger ones when their roots show through at the bottom of the pot. Once they are in their final containers, you need to replenish the nutrients annually in spring by gently knocking out the plants, and teasing away the soil from around the rootball before repotting them in fresh soil in the original container or one similar. Plants too large to repot in this way should have the top 2-3 in of soil replaced annually with a fresh supply.

Container Herb Gardens

Herbs are ideal subjects not only for conventional pots, but also containers of all kinds – wall pots, troughs, window boxes, and anything you have handy, from a battered old sink covered with 'hypertufa' to give it a new lease of life, to a beautiful terracotta chimney pot which can make a centerpiece in an informal cottage garden, especially if you put a few trailing plants around the edge. Containers have advantages of their own: they can be used to confine invasive herbs such as mint, or filled with ericaceous compost for lime-hating plants.

Ocimum basilicum

WINDOW BOXES

A window box makes an ideal herb garden, accessible at all times and changing with the seasons if a supply of potted plants is kept in reserve. Make sure brackets are strong enough to support the weight of moist soil, and use a box about 10-12 in deep to allow a good root run for the plants.

Provide ample drainage in the same way as for other containers, and then fill with a moist soil-based potting mixture. Either plant young herbs directly into this or grow them in 4-5 in pots, burying these just below surface level in the box and replacing them as they are exhausted. Small herbs, especially ornamental varieties, are best but

HERBS FOR A SUNNY WINDOW BOX

- calendula
- dill
- lemon verbena – summer only
- nasturtium – in summer
- sage
- self-heal
- winter savory

- chives
- lemon thyme
- marjoram
- rosemary
- scented-leaved geraniums – summer only
- tarragon

Above: *A strawberry pot may be used not only for strawberries, but also for parsley or any other suitable herb. Always plant as you add the soil, firming each layer into place before filling the next hole.*

Left: *With regular watering and feeding, an ornamental pot on a wall can support alpine strawberries or an ever-bearing large variety that will fruit on trailing runners.*

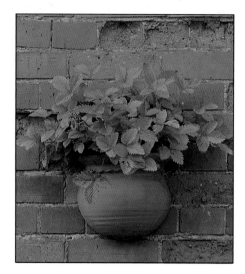

space can be made for taller kinds such as bay and rosemary, started as cuttings and grown in the box until they are too large, when they may be transferred to the garden.

HANGING BASKETS

A hanging basket holds only a small volume of soil and is often exposed to wind and sun from various directions. It needs dedicated attention to watering in hot, dry weather. Nevertheless, many herbs will grow well in a deep basket – seasonal kinds such as basil, nasturtiums and parsley, or permanent decorative crops of pennyroyal, lady's mantle or golden lemon balm. Try growing small-leaved ivies to cascade and cover the sides of the basket, and add a little trailing lobelia or a basket tomato variety for extra flair.

PLANTING IN A STONE TROUGH

1 Protect drainage holes with large stones or curved shards of broken pot and then spread a layer of pebbles or gravel.

2 Fill the trough with a moist, nutritious soil mixture almost to the rim, and help this settle by repeatedly plunging in the trowel.

Above: *Tall, emphatic containers such as chimney pots are perfect for displaying nasturtiums and other climbing or trailing herbs; fill the lower part of the pot with rubble for stability before topping up with soil or compost.*

3 Arrange and plant a few chosen herbs in the trough, but not too many as they will soon fill the available space as they grow.

4 Complete the planting by covering the surface with a decorative mulch of fine gravel or chippings to conserve moisture.

To plant a hanging basket, mix a soil-based medium 50-50 with a soil-less type to reduce weight, and either add a slow-release fertilizer or make sure you feed twice weekly from mid-summer onwards. Suspend the basket out of the wind in a position where you can reach the herbs comfortably for picking and watering. In the autumn transfer the complete basket to a cool greenhouse to prolong the season of use and help plants to survive the winter; the following spring you can take cuttings and remake the basket with fresh soil.

Right: *A stone trough is large enough to house a basic selection of useful herbs or a collection of dwarf species.*

HERBS FOR A LIGHTLY SHADED BOX

- bay
- catmint
- chervil
- corn salad
- mint
- lungwort
- violets

- French sorrel
- chamomile
- chives
- mignonette
- parsley
- salad burnet
- wild strawberry

Herbs Indoors

Herbs are not house plants, and all except the tenderest species need to spend most of their time out of doors if they are to thrive. But many kinds will stand some time indoors without permanent harm, and will add fragrance to your rooms. A pot of basil on an indoor window sill will, when the window is open, release its spicy odor every time the wind stirs the leaves. If you have a conservatory, of course, you can use it for a permanent collection of warmth-loving herbs of all shapes and sizes.

Origanum majorana

HERBS ON THE WINDOW SILL

Apart from shade-loving kinds and a few fleshy-leaved plants such as scented-leaved geraniums, most herbs remain in good condition only for a short time on domestic window sills, and soon suffer from lack of light. The best way to keep a supply of herbs near at hand is to grow several pots of each kind outdoors or in a cold frame or greenhouse, bringing them in one at a time to replace others as these are used up or become drawn and sickly. The superseded herbs are cut back and returned to the frame to revive, or may be planted outdoors after hardening off. All herbs thrive best in the open air, and even long-term pot plants are best moved outdoors in summer. With care, though, it is possible to keep a changing sequence of basic herbs on the window sill throughout the winter, supplemented by lettuce, coriander, and mustard and cress sown direct in pots to give two or three cuts of loose leaves for winter salads.

GROWING UNDER GLASS

In temperate climates a greenhouse or conservatory is essential for growing herbs from warmer parts of the world, and there is a wide enough variety of these to turn a fair-sized greenhouse into an indoor herb garden. Depending on their native habitat, some will be content with minimal frost protection, but tropical species

Above: *A greenhouse or conservatory admits plenty of light to keep plants healthy and compact; except for any in current use, keep potted herbs there where they will remain in good condition until needed.*

Left: *Although many herbs need preserving for out-of-season use, drying subtly alters their flavor and concentration. Parsley, basil, sage, mint and other fresh herbs grown in pots will supply an authentic and stimulating taste of summer.*

will need varying amounts of heat and humidity for good health all the year round. Check cultural needs and build your collection with compatible neighbours – the steamy conditions preferred by a vanilla orchid, for example, would prove lethal to a westringia or grapevine.

Use the walls and roof of the house for training climbers, especially fruiting kinds that will benefit from the good light and a long growing season: in a warm conservatory a fig tree can bear two or three crops of figs a year, compared with only one outdoors. These are best grown in deep containers or in a small soil border. Near the back of the bench arrange large pots of citrus fruit, tea and other greenhouse shrubs, filling the foreground with smaller herbs and trailing varieties to tumble down the front.

Like all pot plants these need regular watering and feeding while in active growth. During the summer paint the glass with shading to prevent sun-scorch and excessively high temperatures. Wetting down the staging and paths with a watering can helps

maintain a healthy atmosphere, and occasionally misting the leaves with water deters red spider mite. If pests and diseases do appear, treat them promptly, as they multiply rapidly in a closed environment. Insect predators are available to control most common pests, while attention to greenhouse hygiene – removing dead flowers and leaves, ventilating freely whenever possible, and maintaining steady growth – will discourage most diseases.

ESSENTIAL HERBS FOR WINDOW SILLS

- basil – sow a pinch in each pot, and prevent flowering for long life; sow again in midsummer for late supplies
- chives – pot up divisions from garden clumps, and keep well fed and watered
- parsley – choose a compact variety, sow in spring and again in late summer for winter cutting; use several pots in rotation
- thyme – start from seed or cuttings rooted direct in the pots; keep in full light and water sparingly

- chervil – sow in spring and again in late summer in quantity in a wide pan, and leave to seed itself when past its best
- marjoram – grow like thyme; choose sweet marjoram for warm rooms, or the hardier pot marjoram where it is cooler
- sage – strike cuttings and keep trimmed frequently; select a variegated kind for indoor color

Above: *Bunches of herbs can remain where they were dried, adding their pervasive scent to the room.*

DIVIDING CHIVES

1 To propagate fibrous-rooted herbs or multiplier onions such as chives, lift a healthy clump and shake off the surplus soil.

2 Gently pull the clump into several pieces; heavy clay soil might need washing off before roots can be disentangled safely.

3 Pot up the divisions in good growing medium, and keep on a warm sunny windowsill for a regular indoor supply.

Pruning and Training

Annual and biennial herbs need little interference with their growth, apart from dead-heading to prolong their lives and seasonal tidying as top growth dies. Herbaceous perennials, too, are largely self-sufficient, although thinning congested growth and cutting their dead flowers to prevent unwanted seeding are often an essential part of their care.

Lavandula spica

Perennial woody herbs, usually need some kind of restraint if they are not to grow too large. In thoroughly prepared ground a contented perennial herb may grow vigorously, a reassuring sign that all is well – although this should not be an excuse for avoiding pruning. Left to their own devices, perennials will continue growing until they reach maximum size, often with unfortunate results such as limited flowering or fruiting and the development of bare stems at the base, while increased competition and overcrowding encourage disease.

Timely pruning will avoid all these complications and banish disorder from the herb garden.

UNDERSTANDING PRUNING

Plants grow upwards and outwards because growth hormones concentrate at the ends of shoots, suppressing the development of buds elsewhere. Cutting off a growing tip redirects the plant's energies to lower buds and stimulates them into growth as replacements for the lost leading shoot. Pinching out the tips of a citrus bush, clipping a lavender hedge and mowing a thyme lawn to remove some of the top foliage are all forms of pruning to limit upward growth and encourage bushy side shoots.

Picking the tips of herb bushes in the course of normal use is a valuable form of basic pruning, but most perennial kinds need one or more overall trims each season to maintain a well-balanced plant. As a general rule, clipping with shears immediately after flowering will restore shapeliness, but this may be done earlier to prevent flowering and allow a longer period of regrowth before the end of the season. A mid-season trim of variegated herbs will provoke a flush of brightly colored new growth; at the same time cut out completely any shoots that revert to plain green. Herb hedges and topiary may need several trims a year, depending on the species used and the degree of strict formality intended.

RENOVATION

Plants such as rosemary, lavender and broom resent being pruned hard, but an annual trim after flowering is essential to maintain size and quality; confine cuts to young green growth, which regenerates freely, unlike older brown stems which may die after

CUTTING BACK

1 Once some herbs are past their best, often after flowering, it is a good idea to cut back their straggly stems almost to ground level.

2 With their long stems removed, young shoots at the base will be exposed to more light and will soon provide a fresh crop of usable leaves.

being pruned. Many other hedge and shrub species, on the other hand, can be cut back hard at the start of the growing season to restore their size. Always check first in a good handbook. Remember, the first rule of pruning is 'Think twice, cut once.'

The most conscientious pruning will not confer immortality on a plant, however, and once a woody perennial such as lavender or sage develops patches of bare stems, it is usually time to start again. Pruning should always be combined with taking cuttings to maintain a stock of available young plants; while these are growing, the older plants can be temporarily restored by hard pruning, layering side shoots of hedge plants to fill gaps, or tying adjacent branches together to disguise dead areas in an important specimen. Always cut out dead and diseased stems when starting pruning or before renovating a plant.

TRAINING

Training accompanies pruning to direct growth in a new direction. Knowing that the topmost bud of a pruned stem is usually the first to break and resume growth allows you to prune back to a bud facing a particular way in the knowledge that the plant will then grow in this direction. Pruning a lax species to upward-facing buds helps prevent it from sprawling too far sideways, while cutting vertical stems to outward-facing buds encourages bushiness.

This technique is particularly useful when training wall shrubs into decorative shapes, since rerouting growth in this way is often safer than attempt-

Right: *The sinuous curves of spiral topiary add a touch of whimsical artistry to a formally designed herb garden.*

ing to bend stubborn branches in a new direction. Some fruits and roses in trained forms need summer pruning to restrain growth and encourage the formation of productive buds, combined with winter pruning to maintain size and shape.

Climbing plants need careful training to prevent them from straggling. They need firm supports on which to climb, or trellis or horizontal wires so that the stems can be tied in evenly as they grow. The annual pruning of many climbers depends on the age of the wood on which flowers are borne – if they bloom on the current year's stems, prune hard in late winter to encourage plenty of young growth; thin this to retain the strongest stems for tying in. Climbers that flower on stems produced the previous year should be pruned immediately after flowering, cutting exhausted stems back to strong new shoots.

Right: *A young mop-head bay, its straight stem trained originally on a firm cane. The dense head of foliage is produced by repeatedly pruning or pinching off the tips of stems to encourage further side shoots.*

Above: *While many hedging and topiary evergreens can be clipped with shears, large-leaved species such as bay need pruning with secateurs or pruners to avoid leaving ugly wounds. Use the prunings as cuttings or for drying.*

Harvesting Herbs

For all their ornamental value, herbs are intended for use, and the dedication that you have put into growing them will be jeopardized by careless harvesting and storage. First establish which parts of the plant are normally used – in most cases it is the leaves and stems, but sometimes the flavour or medicinal value is most concentrated in the seeds, flowers, roots or even bark. Often the concentration is highest at a particular time of year, or even time of day.

Artemisia abrotanum

For routine culinary purposes leaves and sprigs can be picked fresh as needed and whenever available. However, many herbs are not evergreen or accessible all the year round, and it will be necessary at some point to gather larger quantities for preserving and subsequent storage for winter use. Top growth should be harvested when plants are in prime condition and active growth, normally during spring and summer. There is some evidence that oils and active principles are more concentrated in the morning before strong sunlight has affected them, so try to gather material early in the day – but after any dew has dispersed, because damp herbs soon turn moldy. Only gather as much as you can handle immediately from clean, healthy plants, keeping different species separate and clearly labelled.

DRYING LEAVES AND FLOWERS

Living parts of plants contain large amounts of water, as much as seven-eighths of their weight in many cases, and this must be removed before they can be safely stored. In a warm, dry climate, leaves and flowers may be tied loosely together in small bundles and hung in an airy, dust-free place out of the sun until brittle enough to break easily between your fingers (in dusty places enclose bundles in perforated bags). You can also spread them on a table or shelf between sheets of newspaper or muslin, and turn daily, or lay them on a mesh screen raised to allow air circulation beneath. The aim is to retain most of the color, flavor and aroma of the original, so avoid bright

Below: *Freshly gathered herbs in convenient bundles ready for tying and drying.*

sunlight which will bleach the color, and cool conditions that increase drying time with a resulting loss of quality – in most cases a week should be long enough.

In a cool or wet season when natural air drying is not practicable, an airing cupboard, shaded greenhouse, warm attic or dry ventilated shed is an acceptable place. Herbs may be dried in a domestic oven or dehydrator, provided that care is taken to keep the temperature no more than 90°F for the first day or two, after which it can be reduced to 75°F until the process is complete, usually after a further three to five days. Turn the material occasionally and complete one batch at a time – adding fresh material during drying will reduce the temperature and raise humidity. Bunching several herbs together for bouquets garnis will be easier before drying than afterwards.

DRYING SEEDS

Ripe seeds need careful handling because of their natural tendency to shed at the slightest touch. Gather them when they are dry, shaking them from open capsules into paper bags or snipping off complete seedheads, holding them steady as you do so to

Gathering Wild Herbs – a Warning

There are several reasons for taking extra care when harvesting wild herbs, a practice once part of everyday life but no longer easy or even advisable in some districts. Check first that there are no laws or local bylaws against removing plants from the wild (some laws prevent the digging of certain wild flower roots, for example), and as a matter of courtesy always obtain permission from the owner of the land. Pollution is an ever-present hazard, and plants should never be gathered from roadsides and near industrial sites, nor from agricultural land where chemical crop treatments are normally used.

There should be no doubt whatsoever as to the identification of the plants you intend using. Many well-known herbs are unmistakable in appearance or fragrance, but there are also a number of valuable wild herbs which are almost identical to useless or toxic near-relatives. Tasting is a risky identification test and not to be recommended. If you cannot distinguish a plant for certain by its appearance, leave it alone in case it is dangerous. Gather only from plants that are locally plentiful, taking just small amounts of material from any one plant so that its chances of survival are not diminished.

Right: *Bundles of drying herbs need a good circulation of air, for which a suspended drying rack is ideal – but make sure they are kept out of steamy surroundings. The bundles are decorative as well as highly practical.*

Hang up the open bags in an airy place under cover, or spread out seed-heads on paper, leaving them for two or three weeks to finish drying. When seed cases are quite crisp and papery, rub or shake the seeds from their capsules. Some kinds will inevitably be mixed with other plant remains such as broken pods or the aerial 'parachutes' typical of Compositae species, but these can be removed by shaking the seeds in a fine sieve, or simply by gently blowing away the debris.

HARVESTING ROOTS

In most cases roots are dried for storing with their skins intact, but a few such as liquorice, turmeric and marshmallow are best peeled. They are then cut into $1/2$ in slices, thicker roots being cut in two lengthwise. Whether peeled or not, roots take longer to dry than other parts of herbs, often several weeks with frequent turning, but the process can be accelerated in a warm oven set at 120°F. When the fragments are light and brittle, pack them in airtight tins or dark glass jars.

Where the roots of a permanent perennial such as angelica or comfrey are to be harvested, it is best to excavate the soil from one side of the plant and then cut off a few pieces of root with a sharp knife or spade (sometimes a few of these pieces can be used for propagation by potting or boxing them up in soil in the greenhouse). Rub them free of soil and fibrous lateral roots, before taking them indoors to scrub clean. A crop such as horseradish can be grown in a permanent bed, with a root or two being dug as required.

Below left: *Culinary herbs cut up small and packed in measured amounts with water in ice-cube trays lose little of their flavor when frozen, and are ready for almost immediate use.*

Below: *Herbs dried outdoors can be spread in layers if turned regularly, but in still conditions indoors it is better to arrange leaves separately on racks.*

avoid loss. Keep each variety separate and label the bags clearly. If you are saving seeds for sowing, always choose the best plants with typical growth and appearance; inferior plants yield seeds suitable for other uses as long as they are free from diseases. When dry, label and store in packets in airtight jars.

A - Z of Herbs

Achillea millefolium (Compositae)

🐦 **Yarrow**

milfoil, nosebleed, herb militaris, soldier's woundwort, thousand leaf, thousand seal, field hop

Description: hardy herbaceous pungent perennial, 6-24 in. Finely feathered, bright gray-green leaves and flat heads of small white, pink or red flowers midsummer to autumn. Grows in grassy places, including lawns.

Use: folk remedy for rheumatism, toothache, hemorrhage and fever; fresh young leaves used sparingly in salads; herbal tobacco and substitute for hops in brewing.

Cultivation: prefers full sun and well-drained ground; good for chalky and seaside gardens. Spreads readily, so segregate from other plants. Divide roots in spring or autumn, or sow seeds from spring until autumn; plant 6 in apart for lawns.

Parts used: top growth cut just before flowering. Dry outdoors in the shade or in gentle heat indoors.

Related species: *A. decolorans* (English mace): half-hardy perennial, 18-24 in, native to southern Europe. Feathery leaves; yellow flowers, summer. Light soil in full sun.

A. moschata (musk yarrow): rhizomatous perennial, 8 in, from European Alps. Ferny leaves; white flowers, summer. Needs good drain-age and full sun.

Agrimonia eupatoria (Rosaceae)

🐦 **Common Agrimony**

church steeples, liverwort, sticklewort, cockleburr

Description: wayside perennial often found on chalk, 6 in-2 ft. Attractive gray-green cinquefoil leaves, arranged in alternate large and small pairs, with pale yellow star-shaped flowers in summer on tapering spikes like a mullein; apricot scent, popular with bees. Seedheads are burrs which stick to clothes and fur.

Use: once regarded as a magic herb for healing jaundice; used as a spring tonic, as an astringent externally for treating wounds, and in oriental medicine to stop bleeding; a valuable yellow dye plant.

Cultivation: likes well-drained soil in full sun, but will also thrive in short grass. Sow in a seedbed outdoors in spring or autumn, or divide established roots in autumn.

Parts used: whole plant for dyeing; fresh leaves steeped in water to make an infusion; aerial parts except thick stems may be gathered just before flowering for drying gently in the dark; roots may be dried and grated to add to pot-pourri.

Related species: *A. odorata* (fragrant agrimony): highly aromatic plant with sticky, hairy leaves, larger in all parts than *A. eupatoria*. Often planted in wild and woodland gardens.

Ajuga reptans (Labiatae)

🐦 **Common Bugle**

creeping bugle, carpet bugle, carpenter's herb (note that North American bugle, bugleweed or gipsy wort refers to *Lycopus* spp.)

Description: short prostrate perennial, 6 in. Rosettes of coarse shining green leaves, and spires of blue, white or rose flowers in midsummer. Spreads freely by runners. Several cultivated forms including 'Atropurpurea', with metallic purple leaves, and 'Variegata', cream and green, grows best in shade.

Use: medicinally to treat bleeding from cuts and other wounds; popular ground cover among other herbs and for edging containers.

Cultivation: grows in moist, rich soils in shade or full sun; flourishes beneath hedges if compost is added. Sow in spring or autumn in trays and barely cover seed – germination is slow and erratic. Separate established roots and transplant divisions in spring or autumn.

Parts used: leaves picked as required and simmered to make an infusion; whole herb cut down to ground level in summer and dried in shade.

Related species: *A. chamaepitys* (ground-pine, arthritic ivy): short bushy annual with pine scent, 4-6 in. Red-spotted yellow flowers in summer. Whole herb used to treat bleeding and high pulse rate, and in Arab veterinary treatments.

Alchemilla vulgaris (Rosaceae)
🐌 **Common Lady's Mantle**

lion's foot, bear's foot, common alchemil

Description: an aggregate of closely related species, typically herbaceous perennials, 6-18 in. Leaves cloak-shaped and pleated. Small yellowish-green flowers in summer.

Use: used by alchemists in attempts to make gold; folk remedy for eye disorders and to stop bleeding; traditional treatment for menstrual disorders and in childbirth.

Cultivation: grows in sun or shade, in walls, as edging and as ground cover under trees and shrubs, where it self-seeds freely. Sow in trays in summer, and plant out in autumn; or divide clumps in early spring or autumn.

Parts used: leaves and flower shoots picked as required; aerial parts gathered in summer and dried outdoors.

Related species: A. alpina (alpine lady's mantle): evergreen dwarf perennial, grows to 8 in, for sinks, rock gardens and short grass in sun; soft furry, silvery leaves, tiny yellow flowers.

A. arvensis (parsley piert, field lady's mantle): similar to *A. vulgaris*, popular Romany tonic and remedy for bladder stone.

Allium (Liliaceae)

The various species all possess the familiar sulphurous smell, but individually they are valued as vegetables, herbs, medicines and decorative garden bulbs. Only the most important in herbal terms are described here.
Caution: some people are slightly allergic to all forms of onions.

Allium sativum
🐌 **Garlic**

Description: subterranean white-skinned bulb, subdivided into numerous 'cloves'. Short, flat upright leaves, 6-12 in, tall single flower stem bearing spherical head of pale pink or greenish-white blooms often mixed with tiny bulbils.

Uses: flavoring, vegetable and medicinal herb that has accumulated superstitions over the centuries. Used as an antibiotic, expectorant and digestive, and for treating high blood pressure.

Cultivation: cloves planted in autumn 2-4 in deep in rich soil, or in pots in a frame for planting out in spring in cold regions. Harvested in summer when foliage dies down, and dried in sunlight or warmth.

Parts used: bulbs, separated into cloves.

Related species: A. oleraceum (field garlic, wild garlic), *A. triquetrum* (three-cornered garlic), *A. scorodoprasum* (sand leek) and *A. rosea* (rosy garlic) used in various parts of the world as wild substitutes for garlic.

A. ursinum (wild garlic, ramsons): white-flowered wild onion, widespread in damp woodland; pungent garlic smell, but mild when cooked.

A. vineale (wild garlic, crow garlic): wiry version of cultivated garlic, widespread in temperate regions. Used by North American Indians.

Allium schoenoprasum
🐌 **Chives**

Description: small perennial bulb growing in clumps, with fine hollow dark green leaves, 8-12 in, and slightly taller flower stems bearing small clusters of mauve or purple blooms. Can be found wild in moist soils, but usually cultivated.

chives

Uses: mainly culinary for flavoring and garnishing where a mild onion flavor is required. Also a stimulant and digestive; high in vitamin C. Popular decorative herb for edging and for attracting bees. Chive tea is sometimes sprayed to prevent gooseberry mildew and apple scab. Chive flowers can be used in decorative dried flower arrangements.

Cultivation: sow seeds outdoors in spring, or divide clumps into small groups and plant in spring or autumn in moist rich soil. Lift and divide every 3-5 years according to growth. May be potted up in autumn for forcing winter supplies indoors.

(Continued)

Parts used: fresh leaves cut as needed. Chop and freeze in bags or ice-cube trays for use out of season.

garlic chive

Related species: Larger-leaved forms available; also Chinese or garlic chives (*A. tuberosum*) and Siberian chives (*A. schoenoprasum sibiricum*).

Aloe vera, syn. *A. barbadensis* (Liliaceae)

Aloes

Cape aloes, socotrine, medicine plant, burn plant

Description: succulent drought-resistant tropical plant forming clumps of short-stemmed rosettes of fleshy evergreen leaves, up to 2 ft long, pointed and edged with teeth. Tall flower stem with spikes of yellow, orange or red tubular blooms. Often grown as a house plant in cool regions.

Uses: according to legend the sole survivor from the Garden of Eden. Gel-like sap from leaves used externally to heal wounds, burns and mastitis. **Caution:** traditional internal use as purgative bitters ill advised and may cause hemorrhage.

Cultivation: plants need sunny, arid conditions. May be started from seed in spring, or propagated from small offsets at base of parent plant. As house plants, best grown in gritty cactus mixtures in good light; minimum winter temperature of 41°F to ensure flowering, in summer may be stood outdoors. In frost-free gardens, ideal plants for sunny beds with fast drainage.

Parts used: broken leaves rubbed on affected part. Sap extracted from leaves and often dried to form a resin.

Related species: *A. aristata:* small relative with leaves 4-6 in long, white spines and orange flowers. Popular house plant and hardiest of the tropical aloes; may survive mild temperate winters out of doors.

Althaea officinalis (Malvaceae)

Marsh Mallow

guimauve, mortification plant, schloss tea, sweet weed, wymote

Description: tough-rooted herbaceous perennial, 4 ft. Velvety stems and leaves; white or pink flowers in leaf axils in late summer. Found in damp, often saline places.

Uses: valuable and handsome herb with a long tradition of use in medicine and cosmetics, and as a vegetable and confection. Cultivated by the Romans and promoted by Charlemagne. Soothing and mucilaginous; tops of young shoots added to salads (popular with Bedu); flowers and leaves infused to treat lung and bowel disorders; roots sliced and boiled to poultice external inflammation and relieve gastric ailments; root was made into traditional 'marshmallows' (now just sugar and gelatin).

Cultivation: sow seeds in spring indoors in warmth, or outdoors in summer, and transplant to permanent positions in autumn. Roots may be divided in spring or autumn. On light soils mulch freely in summer.

Parts used: flowers, leaves and young tips of shoots gathered fresh; roots at least 2 years old, dug up during winter dormancy when the active constituents are most concentrated, and used fresh or dried.

Althaea Rosea
🐚 **Hollyhock**

Description: biennial or perennial of waste places, and traditional cottage garden flower; grows up to 10 ft. Wide hairy leaves, up to 12 in across. Large flowers, often double, in summer; wild forms are white or pink; cultivated forms purple, red or yellow.

Uses: petals of purple-flowered variety once used to dye wine. Leaves used medicinally as a diuretic and to help some chest complaints. Provides relief for mouth ulcers; soothing to the face.

Cultivation: can be grown in any soil. Propagate from seed and prick out.

Parts used: flowers and leaves, fresh.

Anethum graveolens
(Umbelliferae)
🐚 **Dill**
dillseed, dillweed

Description: annual herb, 18-30 in, with finely feathered blue-green leaves and hollow stems. Small open umbels of creamy-yellow flowers in summer, followed by dark brown seeds. Grows wild in waste places, but can also be cultivated.

Uses: used as a condiment and flavoring and as a pickling spice. Often taken as 'dill water' to relieve digestive problems and flatulence. Occasionally used to perfume cosmetics; medicinal oil distilled from leaves, stems and seeds.

Cultivation: sow in rows or small patches in spring, and again in early summer for continuity, in a sunny, well-drained position. Grow well away from fennel, with which dill cross-pollinates readily. Choose right variety for seed or leaf production.

Parts used: young leaves gathered at any time for use fresh, also flowers for adding to soups; seeds harvested when dry for use whole or crushed. Leaves may be dried, but lose much of their flavor.

Related species: A. sowa (Indian dill, Japanese dill): similar in appearance and uses, popular in Asian cuisines.

Angelica archangelica
(Umbelliferae)
🐚 **Angelica**
garden angelica, Holy Ghost

Description: a robust biennial or short-lived perennial plant, 6 ft, of damp woodlands. Produces a few large, deeply indented leaves at ground level, followed by tall hollow stems bearing from their leaf sheaths heads of green-ish-white flowers in midsummer.

Uses: all parts promote perspiration, stimulate appetite, and are used to treat ailments of the chest and digestion. Young leaves and shoots used to flavor wines and liqueurs, while the stout stems are candied as a cake decoration or cooked like rhubarb. Fresh or preserved roots have been added to snuff and used by Laplanders and North American Indians as tobacco.

Cultivation: sow fresh seeds outdoors in autumn for exposure to frost, or pre-chill in a refrigerator for a few weeks before sowing in spring. Transplant to a moist shady position as young as possible, before the roots become immovable.

Parts used: young leaves can be gathered any time during the growing season, the stems in the summer of the second year. Cut seedheads and ripen until seeds are dry enough to store. Roots are dug up just before flowering and dried slowly.

Related species: A. atropurpurea: a wild North American species used by Shakers as flavoring and medicine.

Anthriscus cerefolium
(Umbelliferae)
೪ **Chervil**
salad chervil, garden beaked parsley

Description: decorative annual, some-times grown as a biennial, 2 ft, with a tapering rootstock. A well-branched plant with sweet-scented and delicate-ly cut pale foliage rather like parsley, and umbels of small white flowers in spring and summer, followed by large seedpods. Sometimes found wild as a garden escape, when it closely resem-bles young cow parsley (*A. sylvestris*). **Caution:** do not gather from the wild, as chervil may be confused with poiso-nous hemlock, fool's parsley and water dropwort.

Uses: leaves used in soups, salads and vinegars, and for garnishes. Medicin-ally the bruised plant is applied fresh or as poultices to wounds; an infusion aids digestion and encourages perspiration.

Cultivation: sow spring, summer or autumn *in situ* in rows or patches, in moisture-retentive soil in full sun or light shade. As plants often run to seed rapidly, sow little and often, or leave plants to self-seed. Sow in warmth for out-of-season supplies indoors.

Parts used: leaves gathered fresh as needed, and frozen or gently dried for storing. Roots sometimes dug and used in salad preparations.

> **Related species:** *Chaerophyllum bulbo-sum* (bulbous chervil): a wild plant with tuberous roots; a close relative of *C. tenuilentum* (rough chervil).

Aquilegia vulgaris
(Ranunculaceae)
೪ **Columbine**
granny's bonnets, European crowfoot

Description: tough-rooted herbaceous perennial with prettily cut leaves on wiry stems, 2 ft. Stout flowering stems in summer bear nodding spurred blooms in white, blue or pink. Found wild in meadows and waste places on chalky soils. Many garden forms with brilliant-colored flowers, often double or with extra-long spurs.

Uses: all parts have been used medici-nally, but now usually grown only as a decorative plant for herb gardens. Roots, flowers and leaves have antisep-tic properties, and roots were once used to treat ulcers. **Caution:** internal use is not recommended as aquilegias contain prussic acid, and all parts are poisonous, especially the seeds.

Cultivation: sow in rows in a nursery bed in late spring for transplanting in autumn; or sow early under glass, and plant out in summer after hardening off. Plant in moist soil in partially shady sites; dead-head garden forms promptly, as self-set seedlings tend to revert to wild form.

Arctium lappa (Compositae)
೪ **Greater Burdock**
beggar's buttons, lappa, cuckoo button, flapper-bags, bardana, clotburr, gipsy's rhizome

Description: short biennial with strong vertical roots up to 3 ft long, and a rosette of large coarse white-backed leaves like rhubarb. In summer thick hairy stems, 6 ft, bear reddish-purple tubular flowers, followed by seedheads (burrs) with hooked spines, lasting all winter. A handsome wild plant of waste places and roadsides.

Uses: a plant of widespread and varied virtues, burdock is cultivated in Japan as a vegetable (*gobo*); used everywhere as a folk remedy for skin problems, especially psoriasis and eczema; grown in China for its seeds, used for throat and chest ailments. A wild vegetable used by North American Indians. The chopped root may be cooked, and the stalks treated like angelica (these con-tain inulin, a mildly sweet substance useful for diabetics). Roots used as flavoring.

Cultivation: usually gathered from the wild, but seeds may be sown *in situ* in rich, loamy soil in the wild garden.

Parts used: roots of 1-year-old plants, split and dried slowly; young shoots and peeled stalks (before flowering) for salads or as a cooked vegetable; dried seeds for medicinal use.

> **Related species:** *A. minus* (common, lesser or small burdock): a similar plant, but with more pointed leaves and smaller seedheads.

Armeria maritima
(Plumbaginaceae)
Thrift
sea pink

Description: evergreen perennial forming mounds of narrow grassy leaves, 4-8 in, on woody rootstock. In early summer produces short-stemmed white or rose flowers with a strong scent of honey. Grows wild in sandy soil beside the sea, but often planted in gardens, sometimes in improved forms.

Uses: an infusion of fresh or dried flowers was formerly used as an antiseptic and to treat nervous disorders, but now thought to cause allergic reactions such as dermatitis. A valuable formal edging plant for herb gardens and for planting in paths; very popular with butterflies.

Cultivation: sow autumn or spring indoors in trays and plant out when hardened off. Tufts may be rooted as cuttings in a shaded frame in summer. Plant in full sun or light shade.

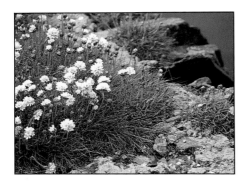

Related species: A. arenaria (Jersey thrift): plant of similar habit but altogether larger, with stout stems bearing deep pink flowers.

Armoracia rusticana, syn.
Cochlearia armoracia (Cruciferae)
Horseradish

Description: coarse herbaceous perennial. Long-stalked oval leaves, up to 3 ft long; umbels of off-white flowers in mid- to late summer. Pungent roots, up to 2 ft long.

Uses: used medicinally as a digestive, antiseptic and stimulant, and to make poultices for rheumatism, chest complaints and circulation problems. Young leaves may be used for flavoring in salads, or cooked; roots are often made into a sauce. **Caution:** use medicinally with care, as the roots may cause internal inflammation, affect the thyroid gland or, used externally, produce blisters.

Cultivation: although often grown as a perennial for occasional use, plants are invasive and virtually ineradicable, every fragment of bought-in root reviving to grow again. Better cultivated as an annual crop by burying 6 in long upper portions of bought-in roots about 12 in apart in ridges of rich soil in early spring. Water well in

dry weather, and in late autumn dig out all the roots for storing in boxes of moist sand.

Parts used: young leaves gathered in spring; roots dug in autumn.

Arnica montana (Compositae)
Arnica
mountain arnica, mountain daisy, mountain tobacco, fall dandelion, leopard's bane

Description: pungent ornamental perennial with creeping rhizomes and prostrate rosettes of downy leaves. Hairy flower stems, 1-2 ft, bear bright yellow daisies in summer and autumn. Grows wild in hilly and highland districts, but also often grown as garden ornamental.

Uses: homeopathic treatment for epilepsy and blood pressure. A formerly popular Shaker salve; used in many countries to treat bruises and sprains, and also for throat infections, wounds and paralysis. Included in some French herbal smoking mixtures. **Caution:** poisonous and not for self-medication, as the plant may be toxic and cause skin irritations.

Cultivation: sow seeds in a cold frame in spring (germination may be slow) and plant out in autumn in sandy acid soils in full sun; divide mature roots in autumn or spring.

Parts used: whole top growth, especially flowers, either fresh or after drying slowly in shade; roots dug up in late spring or autumn and dried in artificial heat.

Artemisia (Compositae)

A large genus of aromatic shrubs and herbaceous perennials, some with finely cut ornamental foliage ranging in color from gray-green to bright silver. Most shrubby kinds are adapted to hot dry places in full sun, and, apart from their medicinal uses, provide valuable color and form in the herb garden. Only the commonest types are described here.

Artemisia abrotanum
Southernwood
lad's love, old man, Crusader herb

Description: graceful woody perennial shrub, up to 3 ft, with pungent feathery leaves, gray-green and downy. Inconspicuous yellow-green daisy-shaped flowers in late summer.

Uses: like all the artemisias, named after the Greek goddess Artemis, who had special care of women. Used medicinally as an infusion or tincture to regulate menstruation, but also as an antiseptic, insect repellent (in mothballs) and air freshener; used by medieval Crusaders to ward off plague. Has a reputation as a hair-wash and bitter stimulant, and even as an aphrodisiac. Stems yield a yellow dye.

Cultivation: prefers to be grown in sun, in well-drained soil. Propagate from soft cuttings in summer, or semi-ripe cuttings with a 'heel' in autumn. Cut back new growth of shrubs by half every spring, and disbud to prevent flowering. An ideal low hedge if trimmed in spring and again in summer.

Parts used: shoots and leaves, which may be dried slowly in the sun.

Artemisia dracunculus
French tarragon
estragon, serpentarian

Description: herbaceous perennial of shrubby growth, with slim woody branching stems 3 ft. Smooth, dark green pointed leaves, and woolly white or grey flowers in late summer. Spreads by creeping rootstocks, which may be invasive.

Uses: popular culinary herb for stimulating the appetite and flavoring sauces, preserves and cooked dishes. Historically used for toothache, and by the Romans to treat snakebite. Useful for catarrhal and digestive problems, while tarragon tea is used to cure insomnia. An ingredient of perfumes and liqueurs.

Cultivation: may only be propagated by dividing the roots in spring or autumn, or from soft cuttings taken in early summer. Grow in rich, well-drained soil and confine roots in the same way as for mint. Renew every three years or so, and mulch in winter to protect roots. Young roots may be potted up for winter supplies but benefit from a dormant period.

Parts used: growing tips gathered for fresh use; all top growth may be harvested at flowering time for drying slowly in gentle heat.

Related species: *A. dracunculoides* (Russian tarragon): a more robust, coarser plant that may be raised from seed, as well as by division and from cuttings. Tolerates a wider range of soil types, but markedly inferior in flavor. Similar uses, but does not dry successfully.

Artemisia vulgaris
Mugwort
felon herb, St John's herb, moxa

Description: herbaceous perennial with red-purple stems up to 6 ft. Long green ferny leaves with white undersides, and numerous reddish-brown flowers in late summer. Com-mon in built-up areas and roadsides.

Uses: one of the nine Saxon magic herbs, used to make a tea for gastritis and digestive ailments, and to treat menstrual disorders. Insect repellent, and ingredient for herbal tobaccos and Chinese treatments for rheumatism. Used in stuffings for fatty meats. Leaves have been used to make fumigant candle wicks, flowers to flavor beer before the advent of hops. **Caution:** may be harmful when taken internally in excessive doses.

Cultivation: may be grown from seeds sown *in situ* in spring and thinned to about 12 in apart, in sun and light shade. Allow plenty of room, as plants grow quickly to full height. Take cuttings in autumn, or divide roots in autumn or spring. Take care that plants do not become invasive.

Parts used: all parts of the plant, either fresh or dried slowly in the shade.

Related species: A. verlotiorum: an Asian wild species, used in Chinese medicine.

Asparagus officinalis (Liliaceae)

🌿 **Asparagus**

sparrow grass, sperage

Description: herbaceous perennial, up to 6 ft. Young, scaly edible 'spears' in spring grow into tall branched stems bearing fine ferny green needles. Greenish-white flowers appear in summer, followed on female plants by red berries in autumn. Fern or 'bower' turns bright yellow as it dies. Found wild on coasts, and widespread in the Middle East; stems may be prostrate.

Uses: an ornamental plant and early summer vegetable. Medicinally used as a laxative, while a tea brewed from the mature fern has been used for rheumatic and urinary disorders, and by Shakers to treat dropsy.

Cultivation: seeds may be sown in rows in spring, the strongest seedlings thinned to 6 in apart; transplant 2 ft apart the following spring in beds or single rows in light rich well-drained soil (on heavy ground create raised beds of suitable soil). Alternatively plant bought 1- or 2-year-old crowns. Start cropping when plants are 3 years old, cutting the 6-8 in high spears just below ground level from spring until midsummer (in parts of Europe the spears are first blanched by earthing up plants). Use largest spears for eating, thinner ones ('sprue') medicinally. Cut down fern and top-dress beds every autumn with compost.

Parts used: young stems ('spears' or 'tips') and fern; roots sometimes dug up for medicinal purposes.

Atriplex hortensis (Chenopodiaceae)

🌿 **Orach(e)**

(red) mountain spinach

Description: an erect leafy annual, up to 2-3 ft or sometimes taller still. Triangular fleshy leaves are dark green, or red in the attractive form *A. hortensis rubra* (red mountain spinach). Thread-like spikes of green or red flowers appear in summer. Common wild on sandy waste land, shingle beaches and salty sites.

Uses: traditional wild herb, often cultivated as a vegetable and garden ornamental; used as a spring tonic and stimulant, and in infusions to treat tiredness or exhaustion.

Cultivation: sow *in situ* in spring in sunny positions, either in rows or broadcast in small patches. Pinch out growing tips once and harvest shoots before plants flower, as they self-seed prolifically.

Parts used: larger leaves and whole young shoots.

Related species: *A. patula* (common orach, ironroot): mealy gray leaves and often trailing stems; common wild on warm beaches, used as a green vegetable.

A. prostrata (hastate orach): similar wild species with much larger leaves.

Borago officinalis (Boraginaceae)

🌿 **Borage**

burage, bugloss, bee bread, bee plant

Description: stout herb, with hollow, bristly stems growing to 2-3 ft. Broad oval leaves, also stiffly hairy, and heavy bent clusters of blue star-shaped flowers (white form occasionally found), popular with bees, followed by oval seed capsules. A cultivated herb, sometimes occurring on waste ground.

Uses: a popular reviver included in some drinks. Young leaves add the flavor of cucumber to salads, older ones can be used as a vegetable, while in France and Italy the flowers are often cooked in batter as fritters. An infusion of leaves and seeds was a folk method of increasing the milk supply of nursing mothers, and to treat coughs, cold and depression. The roots are used to flavor wine, and the seeds are a source of gamma-linoleic acid, an essential fatty acid thought to reduce the risk of arteriosclerosis.

Cultivation: sow in early spring (outdoors or in pots) for flowers the same year, or in late summer outdoors to produce larger biennial plants that flower early the following summer. Grow in well drained soil in full sun. Plants self-seed freely to produce seedlings that usually overwinter safely.

Parts used: leaves and stems (latter said to have greater stimulating properties); flowers used fresh, candied, or dried in moderate heat and kept well sealed; seeds dried for medicinal use; roots dug after flowering.

Buxus sempervirens (Buxaceae)
❧ **Common Box**
boxwood, box tree

Description: a slow-growing evergreen shrub, occasionally small tree, up to 16 ft. Crowded oval leathery leaves, shiny and dark green above, paler beneath. Small greenish-white flowers in mid-spring, male and female blooms in separate groups. Grows wild on chalky commons, but widely cultivated as a garden ornamental, especially as formal hedges since the dense growth tolerates frequent clipping.

Uses: leaves yield a red dye, and are used homeopathically to treat fevers and rheumatism and to promote sweating. One of the best shrubs for topiary and hedges, the compact 'Suffruticosa' being the form grown as dwarf hedging around formal flower and herb beds. **Caution:** the foliage is too toxic for amateur medicinal use.

Cultivation: plant autumn or spring in rich, light soil, preferably in full sun although light shade is tolerated. Keep well watered and feed annually in spring. For hedging choose young plants and space them about 4 in apart, as older ones have very large rootballs and need more space when planted; trim in spring and again at midsummer for formal appearance. Propagate from cuttings outdoors in early autumn, or by layering lower branches.

Parts used: leaves at any time; bark and timber from larger pruned branches.

Related species: B. macowanii (Cape box): very similar species used for the same purposes in South Africa.

Calendula officinalis (Compositae)
❧ **(Pot) Marigold**
common marigold, marybud, marygold, English marigold

Description: perennial herb, usually grown as an annual or biennial, with sticky angular stems up to 2 ft. Long oval leaves, hairy and fleshy, larger at the base; solitary yellow-orange flowers from early summer. Many cultivated forms in a range of yellow, orange and brown, often double.

Uses: apart from being popular old-fashioned cottage garden plants, pot marigolds have a long history of medicinal use. A tea made from the flowers is used for internal spasms and gastric disorders, but the main reputation is as an antiseptic and anti-inflammatory healer of wounds; a common ingredient of many proprietary salves and ointments. Used by Shakers to treat gangrene. Petals can be used as a hair rinse, a coloring agent for butter and cheese, and a substitute for the color of saffron. Also used in cooking and as a garnish.

Cultivation: sow *in situ* in full sun or light shade, in spring for late flowering, or (better) in autumn to overwinter and make bushy plants that flower over a long season the following year. Dead-head regularly to prolong flowering. Although plants thrive best on heavier ground, they tend to self-seed most on light soils.

Parts used: petals fresh or dried in the shade; young fresh leaves in salads; whole flowers boiled as a dye.

Campanula rapunculus (Campanulaceae)
❧ **Rampion**
rampion bellflower

Description: herbaceous biennial with thick fleshy turnip-like taproot, and slim straight angular stems to 3 ft with milky sap. Slim, toothed leaves, oval near plant base; overwinters as a low rosette, producing in the second year pale blue or white star-shaped flowers in midsummer. A wild plant of meadows, fields and hedgerows.

Uses: an ornamental wild flower, whose leaves are used in winter salads. Popular enough in the sixteenth and seventeenth centuries to be cultivated as a root vegetable (but note that 'German rampion' is the root of evening primrose).

Cultivation: for leaves, sow in spring for autumn use, and in early summer for winter crops. For roots, sow in rich soil in a shady position in the kitchen garden, in rows 8 in apart and thin seedlings to the same distance; sow in spring, but if plants flower early in a hot season, sow again in summer.

Parts used: leaves gathered any time before flowering; roots dug from autumn onwards – may be stored in sand in a cool place.

Centaurium erythraea, syn.
Erythraea centaurium
(Gentianaceae)

(Common) Centaury

bitterherb, centaury gentian, feverwort

Description: a delicate annual growing to 12 in, often less. From a rosette of elliptical gray-green pointed leaves, several stems produce branching umbels of tubular flowers in late summer, pink with yellow centers, arranged in clusters and closing when rain is imminent. Found wild in damp meadows and grassy woodlands.

Uses: an ancient Greek and Celtic medicinal herb, used to make a poultice for skin disorders; taken as a bitter tonic by North American Indians. A tea made from the whole plant treats digestive disorders including heartburn, while homeopathic preparation is prescribed for the liver and gall bladder. One of the aromatic ingredients of vermouth.

Cultivation: although growing wild in damp places, it will adapt to most garden soils, thriving and self-seeding in sun or semi-shade in rock gardens and near the sea. Sow in autumn or spring where plants are to grow, and barely cover the seeds.

Parts used: whole plant gathered at flowering time and dried quickly in shade outdoors or in a warm room.

Related species: *C. littorale* (seaside centaury): smaller, with narrower leaves, flower paler but larger. A plant found on sand dunes, with similar uses.

Sabatia stellaris (American centaury): a biennial of marshes and wet localities, with similar uses.

Centaurea nigra

Knapweed

lesser knapweed, black knapweed

Description: tough perennial with sturdy ridged stems and dark green hairy leaves. Grows up to 3 ft. Tubular purple flowers in summer. Grows wild on wasteland, roadsides and as a cliff plant.

Uses: a medieval wound salve; used to soothe sore throats and bleeding gums. Also acts as a diuretic.

Cultivation: grows easily in any soil; needs no particular attention. Self-seeds freely. May need containment.

Chamaemelum nobile, syn.
Anthemis nobilis (Compositae)

Lawn Chamomile

Roman chamomile, double chamomile, common chamomile, perennial chamomile

Description: a vigorous hairy creeping perennial, up to 18 in, with ferny leaves and apple-scented white and yellow flowers in summer; non-flowering forms available for creating lawns. Grows wild in stony ground.

Uses: popular since early Egyptian times, a traditional strewing herb, and often used by Arabs in the form of the essential oil. Ingredient of a famous herb tea for settling nervous disorders, stimulating the appetite and cleansing the blood. Made into herb beers and tisanes, hair rinses and eye lotions, as well as being used in the preparation of cosmetics and perfumes. Essential oil is said to revive cut flowers. Plants often grown as herbal lawns and on ornamental seats.

lawn chamomile

(Continued)

(*Lawn Chamomile* continued)

Cultivation: sow seeds in spring outdoors or under cover, but do not cover as the seeds need light for germination. Established plants may be divided in spring, the only way to propagate named forms. Plant in fertile, well-drained light soil, 18 in apart for specimen plants and 6 in for lawns, and be sure to water well in dry weather.

Parts used: whole plant for distillation; flowers for essential oil and teas, collected as petals begin to reflex in the sun; dried rapidly in shade.

**double
chamomile**

Related species: A. arvensis (corn chamomile), *A. cotula* (stinking chamomile), *Tripleurospermum inodorum* (scentless mayweed): all similar-looking wild flowers with wholly or partly downy leaves, but without the characteristic pleasant subtle apple fragrance.

True wild chamomile is *Matricaria recutita*, q.v.

Chelidonium majus
(Papaveraceae)

🌿 Greater Celandine

swallow-wort, tetterwort

Description: herbaceous perennial with brittle fleshy branching stems up to 3 ft, with soft, finely hairy leaves, yellowish above and blue-green beneath, divided into toothed leaflets. Numerous small yellow flowers appear in summer (double form also available), followed by erect green seed capsules. All parts contain an acrid bright orange sap that may be irritating to the skin.

Uses: once widely grown as a decorative cottage garden herb, but now regarded as a weed of waste and cultivated ground, and walls. Antispasmodic and mildly sedative, traditionally valued for its sap as a treatment for warts and source of an orange dye. Flowers are beneficial for thyroid conditions, while the roots have been used to treat liver and gall bladder disorders. **Caution:** in large doses may be poisonous, and an internal and external irritant.

Cultivation: sow seeds in autumn or divide roots in spring, and plant in dry chalky soils in sun or light shade. Plants normally seed freely but are rarely a nuisance.

Parts used: top growth at flowering time, fresh or dried slowly in darkness; sap at any time from top growth or dormant roots; roots dug in autumn.

Chenopodium bonus-henricus
(Chenopodiaceae)

🌿 Good King Henry

all-good, mercury, poor man's
asparagus

Description: herbaceous perennial with smooth, slightly fluted stems up to 2 ft 6 in, and thick fleshy triangular leaves, gray and mealy at first. Small yellow-green flowers in clusters appear at midsummer. Found wild on light, rich soils, but often cultivated.

Uses: cultivated as an early green spinach-like crop, the first shoots sometimes blanched by earthing up for use like asparagus.

Cultivation: sow in spring *in situ* or in a seedbed, and thin or plant at 18 in distances in light, fertile soil. Plants seed freely, so dead-head to prevent invasiveness.

Parts used: young leaves and shoots.

Related species: C. album (fat hen, common pigweed, common lambs-quarter, white goosefoot): red-stemmed salad ingredient, tonic herb for livestock and source of a red dye; seeds once used for flour.

C. ambrosioides anthelmiticum (American wormseed), Mexican tea: annual wild plant, source of chenopodium oil widely used for the treatment of internal worms. **Caution:** large doses may be poisonous.

C. quinoa (quinoa): Peruvian annual, widely cultivated in South America .

C. botrys (ambrosia), *C. leptophyllum, C. nuttaliae*: other sources of fatty and nutritious seeds.

Chrysanthemum balsamita

&b Alecost

costmary, bible leaf

Description: sharp-tasting herbaceous perennial, growing up to 2 ft. Finely haired creeping rootstock, pale green ridged stems and pointed oval leaves with a minty fragrance. Small yellow flowers often with outer white petals, late summer.

Uses: in medieval times used to ease childbirth; formerly used in brewing as a preservative. Medicinally, used in infusion to soothe colds and digestive disorders. Can be added in small quantities to salads, game, soups and cakes.

Cultivation: sow seed in warm climates, or divide roots and plant in rich, well-drained sunny position. Thin the roots each year. Can also be grown as a pot herb indoors.

Parts used: leaves and flowers; gather young leaves at any time, and flowers as they begin to open.

Cichorium intybus (Compositae)

&b Chicory

succory, witloof, blue sailors

Description: tough herbaceous perennial, sometimes grown as an annual crop, with a large deep taproot that exudes a milky sap, and a basal rosette of long smooth leaves, green and jagged like a dandelion (wild species) or grayish and oval (cultivated forms). Hairy flower stems up to 5 ft bearing bright blue daisies (occasionally white or pink) all summer. A common weed in parts of the USA.

Uses: a vegetable and salad ingredient with a bitter flavor; often forced and blanched (witloof or Belgian chicory) to reduce bitterness. Leaves yield a blue dye. Roots and seeds often roasted as a coffee substitute and additive. Chicory tea used to stimulate bile secretion and to treat gout, rheumatism, anaemia and liver complaints. **Caution:** excessive use can lead to digestive upsets, and handling may cause dermatitis.

Cultivation: sow in rows in late spring in rich soil, and thin to 8 in apart. Roots of witloof varieties are dug in autumn, trimmed to leave a stump of foliage and stored in sand until forced in heat and darkness to produce young buds ('chicons').

Parts used: roots and flowering stems, fresh or dried slowly in the sun; woody core of dried roots discarded before rest is shredded and roasted for coffee; seeds also roasted for drinks.

Related species: C. endivia (endive, escarole): a bitter salad vegetable, with numerous decorative forms, sometimes blanched to reduce bitterness.

Clinopodium calamintha, syn. *Calamintha ascendens* (Labiatae)

&b Common Calamint

mountain mint, mountain balm

Description: hairy herbaceous perennial, with creeping rootstock and bushy growth up to 2 ft. Square stems bear grayish oval, toothed leaves with a mint-like fragrance, and dense branched whorls of lilac or purple flowers in late summer. Found wild in dry waste places, usually on chalk.

Uses: a medicinal plant of ancient Greek and medieval physicians, used in infusions as a tonic and expectorant, and in pleasant mint-flavored tisanes. The whole crushed plant can be used to make poultices for bruises and sprains. Flowers attract butterflies and bees.

Cultivation: sow direct in early spring or autumn outdoors, or in seed trays in autumn to overwinter in a cold frame; germination may be slow and erratic. Alternatively divide mature roots in late spring, or take cuttings from side shoots in early summer. Plant in well drained soil in full sun; will tolerate poor soil.

common calamint

(Continued)

(*Common Calamint* continued)

Parts used: leaves gathered any time, and dried slowly in warmth.

lesser calamint

common calamint

Related species: *C. vulgare*, syn. *Calamintha clinopodium* (wild basil): similar plant with clusters of purple flowers and bristly bracts in summer, and a scent between those of thyme and basil.

C. grandiflorum, syn. *Calamintha grandiflora*: smaller plant, gray-leaved and decorative, with bright lilac flowers in summer.

C. calamintha calamintha, syn. *Calamintha nepeta* (lesser calamint): similar in appearance and uses to common calamint, with grayer leaves and almost white flowers.

Cnicus benedictus, syn. *Carduus benedictus* (Compositae)

🐦 Holy Thistle

blessed thistle, spotted thistle, St Benedict thistle

Description: branching annual with a single taproot, hairy, reddish stems up to 2 ft, and long white-veined green leaves, deeply cut and spiny. In late summer thistle heads of yellow flowers and brown bracts appear, almost enclosed in a tuft of small leaves and followed in autumn by fat achenes (single seedpods).

Uses: ancient remedial herb used as digestive tonic, to treat liver and gall-bladder complaints, and to induce sweating. A poultice of the leaves relieves chilblains, wounds and burns. Roots used in aperitifs and may be boiled as a vegetable, flowerheads sometimes eaten like globe artichokes.

Cultivation: usually found wild, but may be sown in spring or autumn in patches *in situ*, or for transplanting to loose fertile soil in full sun. For crops sow in rows 18 in apart.

Parts used: roots dug just after flowering; leaves picked before flowering and dried slowly; flowers used whole; seeds gathered when dry.

Convolvulus arvensis (Convolvulaceae)

🐦 Field Bindweed

lesser or pink bindweed, cornbine, devil's guts

Description: climbing or scrambling herbaceous perennial, with twining stems up to 3 ft long and deep, often tightly coiled rhizomatous roots. Leaves neat and arrow-shaped with basal lobes, in summer and autumn white (or pink on soils rich in iron) funnel-shaped flowers. Difficult to eradicate.

Uses: a tonic and blood cleanser, sometimes used in infusion for fevers and constipation. The flowers may be added to salads.

Cultivation: rarely necessary, but may be propagated from stolons and planted in full sun.

Parts used: flowering top growth, fresh or dried.

Related species: *C. floridus*: North American species whose roots and stems are dried and ground into fragrant *bois de rose*.

Calystegia sepium, syn. *Convolvulus sepium* (hedge bindweed, bellbine): much stronger growing than field bindweed, up to 10 ft, with large white flowers.

Coriandrum sativum
(Umbelliferae)
Coriander
cilantro

Description: rigid, strong-smelling annual with pronounced taproot, and slender stems up to 2 ft. Ferny pinnate leaves, rounded and parsley-like at base, and umbels of small white or pink flowers in midsummer, followed by round red-brown seed capsules, aromatic when ripe. Many named forms selected for leaf or seed production; small-seeded varieties are usually grown in temperate regions, large-seeded kinds in warmer climates. Grows wild in bare places, usually as an escape from cultivation.

Uses: one of the oldest recorded spices, mentioned in ancient Sanskrit texts and in Exodus (coriander is one of the bitter Passover herbs). The leaves and shoots are added to salads, soups and stews, especially in India, South America and China (the leaf is sometimes known as 'Chinese parsley'). The seeds are a stimulant and digestive, often ground and included in curries and regional meat dishes. They are used as a flavoring for bread, and yield an essential oil for soaps and perfumes. They are sometimes added to pot-pourri, and to other herbs to disguise their unpalatability. The root supplies a stronger flavoring, and is often cooked as a vegetable in South-East Asia.

Cultivation: sow *in situ* in autumn or spring, and thin to 6 in apart. Grows fast in full sun, in well-drained soil with a little lime. Protect the brittle stems from wind. Plants usually self-seed freely. Several sowings are advisable for good leaf production.

Parts used: young leaves and shoots at any time; mature seeds dried, roasted and pulverized before use; roots dug after flowering.

Cymbopogon citratus (Gramineae)
Lemon Grass
oil grass, takrai, sereh

Description: coarse tufted tender perennial grass, lemon-scented, with strong roots and spear-shaped, brownish-green leaves up to 3 ft, growing from a tough, fibrous bulbous base.

Uses: leaf buds and chopped stems are added to oriental dishes, and made into a tea for liver complaints. The plant yields lemon-grass oil, rich in vitamin A, which is used as a tonic and stimulant, antiseptic, and oily skin cleanser, as an ingredient of cosmetics, and as an aromatherapy oil.

Cultivation: divide clumps and plant offsets with their bottom 1 in buried in rich soil in a warm, sunny site sheltered from cold winds.

Parts used: leaf buds; stems fresh and finely chopped, or dried and ground.

Related species: *C. flexuosus* (Indian lemon grass): an alternative source of lemon-grass oil and an antiseptic.

C. martinii (ginger grass): a source of ginger-grass oil and palma-rosa oil.

C. nardus (citronella grass): yields Ceylon citronella oil for perfumery.

Cynara cardunculus
Cardoon

Description: a close relative of the thistle and globe artichoke, this short-lived perennial grows up to 6 ft. Impressive silvery leaves, ridged stems, often grown as an ornamental garden plant. Gray-blue thistle-like flowers appear in late summer.

Uses: an ornamental garden favorite, also an edible vegetable crop with a delicate flavor. Especially popular in Mediterranean countries. Best eaten in winter and spring.

Cultivation: from seed in almost any soil. To increase yield, cut down to ground level in early summer, feed and water copiously. New growth will be produced until well into autumn.

Parts used: stems, blanched, braised or fried; also added to sauces.

Cynoglossum officinale
(Boraginaceae)

&. Hound's Tongue

gipsy flower, rats-and-mice

Description: hairy gray-green herbaceous biennial, smelling of mice, with stems up to 3 ft. Leaves roughly hairy, large and oval or tongue-shaped near base of plant, upper ones much narrower. Clusters of hooded flowers, dull maroon or occasionally white, appear in midsummer, followed by hard, flat fruits covered with short-hooked spines. A wild plant of dry, grassy areas, especially near woods.

Uses: infusion from shaved root or crushed leaves used to bathe cuts, bruises, burns and eczema, and to treat coughs and bronchitis; leaves produce a potent poultice for external relief. A nectar-rich plant for bees and butterflies. **Caution:** self-medication is not recommended, as internal use can be dangerous, and external applications may cause dermatitis.

Cultivation: usually gathered from the wild, but seeds may be sown in late summer *in situ*: these need frost to stimulate germination and will not appear before the following spring. Grow in light, well-drained soils in full sun. Plants succeed in seaside gardens, and self-seed freely.

Parts used: flowers and leaves, fresh or dried in shade or a warm room; root fresh or dried.

Related species: C. germanicum (green hound's tongue): a similar plant, with leaves shiny and hairless, and lacking the distinctive odor of *C. officinale.*

Dianthus caryophyllus
(Caryophyllaceae)

&. (Clove) Pink

(clove) gillyflower, carnation, sops-in-wine, divine flower

Description: an evergreen perennial with gray-green branched stems 2-3 ft divided into sections by hard knuckles or nodes, from which long, thick gray-green waxy leaves, stiff and smooth-edged, arise in pairs often joined at their base. Showy, very fragrant flowers, rose-pink or white, appear in summer and early autumn. Found wild on walls and in chalky places in warm climates; cultivated in numerous forms and colors, especially as perpetual-flowering and border carnations.

Uses: an outstanding ornamental plant, whose fresh flowers are used in tonics, and to flavor drinks and syrups; dried petals are often added to potpourri.

Cultivation: easily grown on light, well-drained chalky soil in full sun. May be raised from seed sown under glass in spring, the seedlings potted on or transplanted outdoors to a nursery bed for planting in autumn. Propagate named forms from pipings in summer, or cuttings with a heel in early autumn.

Parts used: flowers, fresh or dried. Before culinary use remove the bitter petal base.

Related species: D. plumarius (cottage pink, grass pink): smaller plant with slender rough-edged leaves, and fringed flowers in white, pink or purple; one of the parents of the garden pink.

Dryopteris filix-mas

&. Male Fern

Description: a fern with large fronds which grow up to 4 ft. Veins on the underside of fronds are covered with sporangia. Grows in damp woodlands and in hilly and mountainous areas.

Uses: once used to expel tapeworms, and formerly believed to soothe wounds, cure rickets and ease rheumatism. **Caution:** recent research suggests many species of fern are carcinogenic; male fern should be avoided; it should never be taken internally, especially not by those suffering from cardiac problems or by pregnant women.

Cultivation: grows freely in damp areas and on hedge banks. Should be avoided in the herb garden because of possible health risks.

Echium vulgare (Boraginaceae)

Viper's Bugloss

blue weed, blue devil

Description: herbaceous biennial with an exceptionally long drought-resistant taproot and coarse, hairy stems up to 3 ft. Grayish freckled leaves, long and narrow with rounded tips near the base of the plant, shorter on the flowering stem. Plants flower at midsummer, the dense panicles of pink buds opening into bright blue flowers with long, conspicuous stamens. A wild plant of dry, stony or grassy places, often near the sea; cultivated blue or white forms grown in gardens.

Uses: an outstanding ornamental plant, originally used to treat snakebite (both the seeds and stem markings resemble the features of snakes), the whole plant being crushed and applied to the bite. Flowers are mildly tonic and antiseptic, and may be added to drinks or candied. Leaves may be cooked like spinach.

Cultivation: sow in late summer in any soil where plants are to flower, and thin seedlings to 18 in apart; transplant others to new sites while still young and their taproots undeveloped. Plants self-seed freely where happy.

Parts used: fresh young leaves and shoots before flowering; flowers when fully open.

Related species: E. lycopsis (purple viper's bugloss): more softly hairy, with larger red-purple flowers and fewer stamens. Similar uses.

Eruca vesicaria spp. *sativa* (Cruciferae)

(Garden or Sweet) Rocket

rocket-salad, rocket-gentle, rocquette

Description: fast-growing annual, with a rosette of smooth, dark green leaves, indented like a dandelion. Branched, leafy main stems, hairy and reddish, growing to 2 ft, producing sparse simple flowers of loose, floppy creamy-yellow petals with purple veins, followed by fat, crisp seedpods.

Uses: salad herb with pungent flavor, especially popular in Mediterranean countries. A tonic, mild stimulant and cough remedy. Crisp seedpods are edible, seeds used to treat bruises and supply mustard oils.

Cultivation: for succulent leaves grow in rich, moist soil in full sun or light shade; on hot, dry soils plants run to seed quickly and produce tough, bitter leaves. Sow in spring and again at midsummer (all year round in warm districts), and keep well watered. Plants usually self-seed.

Parts used: leaves gathered in succession as soon as plants are large enough; seedpods while young and juicy; seeds from ripe seedpods.

Eupatorium perfoliatum (Compositae)

Boneset

thoroughwort, agueweed

Description: perennial herbaceous herb, with branching rough stem up to 5 ft. Long narrow pointed leaves, dark green and shiny above, and white and downy beneath. Dense heads of small white, occasionally blue, flowers, followed by feathery seedheads.

Uses: a popular tonic and stimulant, best known as a hot infusion for treating coughs and colds, or as an ointment or syrup for muscular aches.

Cultivation: sow on the surface of seed trays in autumn or spring in a cold frame; divide mature plants in spring or autumn, and grow in damp or marshy soil in sun or light shade.

Parts used: whole plant as flowers open, fresh or dried quickly in warmth.

Related species: E. ayapana: Brazilian species, producing a stimulant and digestive tea.

E. cannabinum (hemp agrimony, water hemp): contains eupatorin, used to treat dropsy; flowering herb or root also used as a tonic and laxative.

E. purpureum (joe-pye weed, gravel-root, queen of the meadow): white- and purple-flowered plant up to 10 ft; North American Indian red dye plant; roots and seedheads used to treat rheumatism, backache and urinary disorders.

Filipendula ulmaria, syn. *Spiraea ulmaria* (Rosaceae)

❧ **Meadowsweet**

queen of the meadows, meadsweet, meadwort

Description: herbaceous perennial with a pink aromatic creeping rootstock. Reddish stems, up to 4 ft, bear pinnate leaves. Dense panicles of fragrant, creamy-white flowers in late summer.

Uses: an early source of salicylic acid. Tea from the flowers reduces fever, and is used to treat stomach acidity, influenza and rheumatism. Flower buds produce oil for perfume, and the dried flowers are added to home-made wines. Leaves flavor drinks, especially beer and mead. Dyes made from the roots (black) and flowers (yellow).

Cultivation: sow in spring or autumn *in situ* or in trays of compost under glass, or divide roots in spring. Plant in moist, rich soil in sun or light shade.

Parts used: flowers fresh or dried gently in warmth; roots dried for homeopathic use; leaves for flavoring.

Related species: *F. vulgaris* (dropwort): smaller plant, up to 2 ft, with less dense flowerheads. Roots sometimes used as a vegetable.

F. rubra, syn. *F. magnifica* (queen of the prairie): similar North American species with pink flowers.

Foeniculum vulgare (Umbelliferae)

❧ **Fennel**

spigel

Description: grayish-green, strong-smelling herbaceous perennial, with slim stems up to 6 ft, bearing soft lacy, dark green leaves with thread-like lobes and swollen bases. Creeping rootstock gradually extends plant into a sparse clump. Small mustard-yellow flowers appear in summer, followed by small egg-shaped seedpods. Grows

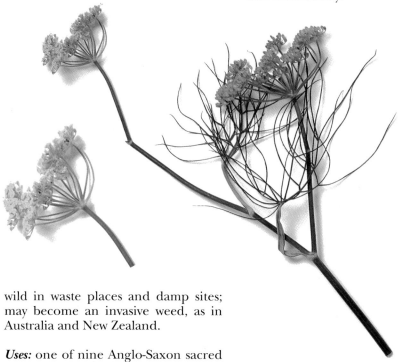

wild in waste places and damp sites; may become an invasive weed, as in Australia and New Zealand.

Uses: one of nine Anglo-Saxon sacred herbs; much used by ancient Greeks and throughout the Middle Ages. Roots once boiled as a vegetable, and used as an expectorant in cough mixtures. Dried stalks are an essential ingredient of Provençal cuisine. Soft growing tips are widely used to flavor and garnish fish dishes, soups and baked foods, and may be made into fennel tea to treat indigestion and colic. A popular flavoring for liqueurs and a scent for soaps and cosmetics. Oil produced from seeds is antibacterial. In warmer regions foliage attracts swallowtail butterflies. **Caution:** avoid large doses.

Cultivation: for lavish growth light, moist soils are best. Divide roots in spring and plant in a warm sunny place, or sow seeds in spring or summer, either in pots or *in situ* 20 in apart. Roots become long and tough,

so transplant while still young. Water well in dry weather. Fennel self-seeds freely, so dead-head if seeds not needed. Plants become congested and exhausted after 3-4 years, and are then best replaced. Do not grow near dill, as these two species cross-fertilize readily to produce useless hybrids.

Parts used: growing tips, fresh or dried in early summer (leaves and stems may be cropped several times before flowering); seeds, from seedheads cut in autumn before fully mature and dried in warmth; roots dug in autumn and dried slowly.

Related species: *F. vulgare* 'Dulce' (Florence fennel, finocchio, sweet fennel): annual cropped from the wild for its essential oil, and cultivated as a vegetable for its juicy, swollen stem base.

F. vulgare 'Piperitum' (carosella, cartucci): local Italian vegetable with blanched young stems.

Ferula foetida (asafoetida): perennial herb used as an Indian condiment and in sauces; medicinal resin extracted from the root.

Ferula galbaniflua (galbanum): Middle Eastern species, the stem and roots of which yield an aromatic gum used for incense.

Fragaria vesca (Rosaceae)

🌿 **(Wild) Strawberry**

wood strawberry

Description: deciduous herbaceous perennial, spreading by runners or stolons. Single white flowers on stems in summer, followed by red or white berries with numerous yellow seeds on the outside. Grows wild in woods and grassy places on dry soil.

Uses: mildly laxative fruits are a nerve tonic, rich in iron. Leaves can be made into a popular tea that is a diuretic and astringent; fresh leaves sometimes added to salads. **Caution:** excessive consumption sometimes leads to allergic reactions.

Cultivation: plant young runners in spring or autumn, or sow seeds under glass in spring (sow on the surface and keep moist – germination may be slow and erratic). Plant in sun or light shade, in any soil except clay.

Parts used: fruit when fully colored; leaves at any time; roots dug in winter.

Related species: *F. moschata* (hautbois strawberry, musk strawberry): wild species with larger flowers.

F. virginiana (wild strawberry): red-fruited wild species, an important North American Indian legendary and medicinal plant, and one parent of most large-fruited forms.

Galium odoratum, syn. *Asperula odorata* (Rubiaceae)

🌿 **(Sweet) Woodruff**

kiss-me-quick, master of the woods (Waldmeister)

Description: herbaceous perennial, often evergreen. Branched stems up to 12 in bear neat whorls of dark green leaves. Clusters of star-shaped flowers on long stalks appear in early summer.

Uses: flavors wines and other drinks, and scents linen, pot-pourri and perfumes. Medicinally used to poultice wounds and scabies, and to stimulate milk flow of nursing mothers. **Caution:** excessive use may produce dizziness and respiratory allergies.

Cultivation: divide roots at any time, or sow ripe seeds in late summer *in situ.* Grow in rich, alkaline soil in shade, and harvest from second year onwards.

Parts used: green plant cut at or just before flowering time, and dried slowly.

Related species: *G. verum* (lady's bed-straw): taller and with thinner leaves; sweet-scented yellow flowers used to curdle milk and color cheese; stems yield a red dye.

Asperula tinctoria (dyer's woodruff): white-flowered species, giving a yellow-orange dye.

Gaultheria procumbens (Ericaceae)

🌿 **Wintergreen**

partridge berry, tea berry, chequerberry

Description: evergreen perennial shrub with prostrate creeping stems from which erect branches grow to 6 in high. Top of each branch bears a few leathery, serrated oval leaves, shiny and paler beneath. Drooping white or pink flowers appear in midsummer, followed by pea-sized scarlet berries. A wild plant growing in woodlands on acid soils.

Uses: leaves made into aromatic infusion for use as a gargle. Leaves are pain-reducing, and when dried can be made into a tea. Oil distilled from the leaves rubbed in externally to treat muscular aches and pains, and also used to flavor dental preparations.

Cultivation: excellent ground-cover plant for moist, acid soils and rock gardens. Plant in autumn or spring in peaty soils in full sun or light shade. Propagate by seeds sown in a seedbed outdoors in autumn, or from rooted prostrate stems in spring.

Parts used: leaves fresh or dried in the sun, distilled for oil of wintergreen.

Related species: *G. antipoda*: New Zealand species, either prostrate or a medium-sized shrub, with edible red berries.

G. shallon (shallon, salal): vigorous, shrubby North American species, with purple berries.

Genista tinctoria (Leguminosae)

Dyer's Greenweed

dyer's broom

Description: dwarf deciduous broom-like shrub, sometimes prostrate or erect to 3 ft. Bright green branches and narrow pointed glossy leaves; long, leafy racemes of bright yellow pea-type flowers in summer. A wild plant of dry grassy places and heaths; numerous cultivated forms, including one with double flowers.

Uses: a decorative ground-cover plant to grow with heathers. Infusion made from young flowering shoots is diuretic and laxative, and used to treat dropsy and skin disorders. Young flower buds may be pickled like capers. Flowers yield a yellow dye, rich green if mixed with woad.

Cultivation: poor soil in an open, sunny position with good drainage is ideal. Plant autumn or spring, or sow seeds outdoors in autumn after rubbing them between sheets of sandpaper; named varieties may be grafted on to laburnum rootstocks in spring. Prune soft growth after flowering.

Parts used: flower buds; flowers for dye; young flowering shoots fresh or dried in shade.

Geranium maculatum (Geraniaceae)

American Cranesbill

spotted cranesbill, alum root, crowfoot

herb robert

American cranesbill

Description: hairy herbaceous perennial with stout rhizomatous root and stems up to 2 ft. Leaves elegant and downy, divided with scalloped edges and blotched with white as they age. Small pink-purple, occasionally white, flowers appear in late spring, followed by fruits with long barbs like the bill of a crane. A wild plant of hedgerows and woodlands.

Uses: a popular North American Indian herb; root is astringent, used in infusions or as a powder to treat diarrhoea, dysentery and bleeding, and ulcers, both internal and external.

Cultivation: divide mature plants in early spring, or sow in autumn or spring where plants are to grow after rubbing seeds between sheets of sandpaper. Grow in full sun or light shade in moist, leafy soil. Plants self-seed profusely and soon develop into thick clumps.

Parts used: roots gathered in autumn or winter, dried and powdered.

Related species: G. robertianum (herb robert, stinking cranesbill): annual with pink or white flowers; whole plant (including roots) is a powerful wound herb, used to stop bleeding and heal oral inflammations.

Geum urbanum (Rosaceae)
❧ **Herb Bennet**
wood avens, clove root

Description: downy herbaceous perennial with strong thick aromatic pink root and branched stems up to 2 ft. Grows as a rosette of dark green oval leaflets of unequal size, the terminal one largest, toothed or deeply lobed. In summer and autumn bears loose open panicles of yellow flowers. A wild plant of woods and shady fertile places, and 'weed' of cultivated soil.

Uses: spicy root, a medieval pot herb and substitute for cloves, can be made into an infusion for stomach and liver disorders, to increase appetite and stop bleeding, or into a strengthening tea to reduce fever; also used as a mouthwash. Young leaves can be eaten in salads.

Cultivation: sow in spring or autumn where flowers are to grow, and thin to 6 in apart. Grow in fertile soil in full or semi-shade.

Parts used: roots fresh or dried in shade or warmth; young leaves.

Related species: G. rivale (water avens, Indian chocolate): delicate perennial with trefoil leaves and nodding bell-shaped pink flowers, preferring damp shade or the margins of ponds. Similar uses, but milder in effect; also used to make chocolate-flavored drinks.

Glycyrrhiza glabra (Leguminosae)
❧ **Liquorice**
licorice, sweet root

Description: vetch-like herbaceous perennial, with long yellow fibrous taproot, numerous subroots and creeping stolons. Stems to 5 ft, bearing pale green pinnate leaves with small oval leaflets in pairs. From the leaf axils loose, conical lilac-blue pea-type flowers appear in midsummer, followed by long brown seedpods.

Uses: cultivated for its sweet aromatic roots since the Middle Ages; used by Arab physicians as a laxative, and for treating stomach problems such as ulcers, and bladder and kidney complaints. Infusion given for bronchial catarrh and sore throats, and to reduce fever. Popular sweetener and flavoring for confectionery, beers and tobacco. Waste fibers after processing used to make wallboard. **Caution:** long-term use can raise blood pressure, lower potassium levels and lead to sodium retention.

Cultivation: grow in deep, well-drained soils in full sun. Divide roots in spring and plant 4 in deep and 18 in apart. Cut down foliage annually in autumn and remove any creeping stolons.

Parts used: roots from 3-4-year-old plants, dug in autumn or spring, peeled and dried; juice may be extracted from fresh roots.

Hamamelis virginiana (Hamamelidaceae)
❧ **(Common) Witch Hazel**
winterbloom, spotted alder

Description: deciduous perennial shrub or small spreading tree with smooth pale bark, up to 13 ft. Small elliptical hazel-like leaves, downy when young, and ragged spidery bright yellow flowers on bare stems from late autumn onwards. A wild shrub of damp woods and watersides, widely grown as an ornamental and rootstock for cultivated witch hazels.

Uses: traditional astringent and cooling wound herb, sacred to North American Indians. Made into an infusion for treating bruises, sprains, varicose veins and bleeding, and an ointment for relieving piles. Commercial witch hazel is made from young flowering twigs. **Caution:** tinctures made from the leaves and bark may cause allergic reactions.

Cultivation: prefers lime-free soils in full sun or light shade, may be grown as a decorative lawn specimen or among other shrubs, or trained against walls. Sow seeds in spring in trays under glass or a seedbed outdoors, or layer branches in autumn. Cut out suckers annually; if rooted these may be transplanted for new plants.

Parts used: bark and leaves for tinctures; flowering twigs for distillation.

Hedera helix (Araliaceae)

Ivy

English ivy

Description: long-lived evergreen climber, with woody stems clinging by aerial roots, up to 100 ft. Dark green glossy leaves, often with paler veins; juvenile foliage pointed and lobed, often palmate. When stems reach full light they branch freely and bear smaller simple pointed oval leaves and globular heads of greenish fragrant flowers in autumn, followed by black berries. A wild plant growing in trees and hedges or prostrate on shaded soil; numerous ornamental forms.

Uses: once regarded as a protective magical plant, with numerous internal medicinal uses: berries were taken as a purgative, and leaves used to treat fevers and glandular disorders. They may safely be turned into an effective poultice for bruises and stiff joints. Plants produce a resin sometimes included in varnishes; flowers attract bees, and birds depend on the berries in winter. **Caution:** whole plant is poisonous and should be restricted to external use.

Cultivation: plants prefer rich, well-drained soil in full or semi-shade. Sow in autumn, exposing seed trays to frost over winter, or use pieces of stem bearing aerial roots as cuttings. Peg shoots to soil surface at first to encourage more rapid growth and coverage of walls. Prune in spring, trimming off old leaves and shortening or removing any unwanted straggly stems.

Parts used: young leaves, fresh or dried in shade.

Helichrysum italicum, syn. *H. angustifolium* (Compositae)

Curry Plant

everlasting flower, helichrysum

Description: evergreen aromatic bush with branched woody stems up to 2 ft. Fragrant narrow, silvery-white leaves; rich yellow daisies on long stalks in summer.

Uses: intensely aromatic herb for flavoring meat dishes, drinks and jellies, and effective as an insect repellent. Essential oil used in cosmetics, and for treating respiratory problems.

Cultivation: grow in poor soil in a sunny, well-drained position, protected from frost and cold winds in winter. Divide plants in spring, take cuttings from side shoots in summer, or sow under glass in spring. Plant in autumn or spring; in formal positions trim off flowering stems as these detract from the foliage, but never cut into old wood.

Parts used: leaves; flowers in bud dried for arrangements; flowerheads and shoots in summer for distillation.

Related species: *H. cochinchinense*: South-East Asian species, leaves used to flavor rice dishes.

H. serpyllifolium, syn. *Plecostachys serpyllifolia*: South African species, leaves made into tea.

H. stoechas (goldilocks): bright yellow-flowered dwarf shrub; leaves used as a vermifuge.

Humulus lupulus (Cannabinaceae)

Hop(s)

Description: hairy aggressive perennial climber, with long spreading stolons and twining stems ('bines'), often twisting around each other into ropes, up to 30 ft. Leaves heart-shaped or palmately lobed, with toothed edges. Clusters of greenish male and female flowers appear on separate plants in summer, female flowers ripening into large cones of overlapping bracts in autumn. Grows wild in hedges, cultivated commercially and grown as a garden ornamental.

Uses: common flavoring and antibacterial preservative in beer; female cones used to treat insomnia and nervous tension, and included for their hormonal content in skin creams and lotions. Hop poultices applied to boils and swellings. Young shoots and leaves cooked as vegetables; fibers from the stems are used in the textile industry.

Cultivation: grow from cuttings or divisions from the base of the plant in spring, or sow seeds in late summer and autumn in a cold frame. Plant in rich, moist soil in full sun or light shade, and grow up sturdy tall supports. Mulch in spring with rotted manure, thin young shoots to 5-6 per crown, and water freely in dry weather.

Parts used: female cones gathered in early autumn while still green, and dried until brown, sometimes powdered; young shoots 6-8 in long in spring.

Hypericum perforatum (Guttiferae)

੨ (Perforate, or Common) St John's Wort

Description: low evergreen perennial, with long, wiry runners or stolons and branched stems up to 3 ft, woody at base and marked with two raised parallel lines. Small, pale green leaves arranged in opposite pairs and speckled with translucent dots, which are oil glands. Bright yellow flowers appear in late summer, petals edged with black dots. A wild plant of grassy and shady places, usually chalky.

Uses: leaves mildly sedative, and stimulate gastric and bile secretions. Sometimes used to treat poor blood circulation and irregular menstruation, but best known as an antibacterial remedy for slow-healing wounds and burns. Young leaves eaten in salads; flowers yield red and yellow dyes. **Caution:** avoid exposure to the sun during treatment, as the plant causes photosensitivity.

Cultivation: grow in sun or light shade in well-drained soil. Divide roots in spring, take cuttings in summer, or sow seeds in trays in spring. Plant in autumn or spring, and prune damaged stems after frosts.

Parts used: young leaves and flowers fresh or dried in shade.

Related species: *H. androsaemum* (all-heal, tutsan): larger, shade-loving plant with unspotted leaves and black berries in autumn; a noted wound herb.

Hyssopus officinalis (Labiatae)

੨ Hyssop

Description: perennial evergreen shrub with branching stems up to 2 ft. Long narrow green fragrant leaves, hairy and dotted with oil-bearing glands; whorls of blue, pink, purple or white flowers on long narrow spikes in autumn, popular with bees. A wild plant of dry stony soils on chalk, and an ornamental herb, sometimes used for dwarf hedging.

Uses: a valuable expectorant; flowering tips infused in water used to treat coughs and sore throats, also to heal bites, burns and stings. Often added for flavoring to soups, stews and salads. Distilled oil used in liqueurs and perfumes.

Cultivation: grow in full sun in well-drained, light soil. Sow in spring under glass, take cuttings in early summer, or divide in spring or autumn. Plant 8 in apart for hedging and clip to shape in spring.

Parts used: leaves fresh at any time; flowering tips fresh or dried in sun.

Related species: *Agastache foeniculum* (anise hyssop): aromatic herbaceous perennial, dried leaves used for seasoning and teas.

A. urticifolia (nettle-leaved giant hyssop): herbaceous perennial, used by North American Indians medicinally and as flavoring.

Isatis tinctoria (Cruciferae)

੨ Woad

dyer's weed

Description: biennial or short-lived perennial, with basal rosette of long-stalked, oval toothed leaves, blue-green and downy, with branched leafy stems up to 4 ft, stem leaves smaller, sessile and arrow-shaped. Graceful loose panicles of small yellow flowers in early summer, followed by pendulous black seeds. A wild plant of waste places on chalk, widely cultivated until this century.

Uses: an ancient dye and healing plant, fermented leaves producing a blue dye eventually superseded by indigo. Leaves were also traditionally used to stop bleeding and heal the wounds of battle. **Caution:** for external use only.

Cultivation: grow in full sun in well-drained, rich chalky soil. Sow *in situ* in late summer and thin seedlings to 12 in apart. Removing stems before they can flower extends the life of plants, which will otherwise seed themselves freely as biennials.

Parts used: leaves repeatedly fermented and dried in a complicated sequence of operations.

Juniperus communis
(Cupressaceae)
Juniper

Description: evergreen coniferous shrub or tree, prostrate or upright to 20 ft. Needle-like leaves, prickly and emitting scent of apples if bruised. Yellow-green flowers in early summer, followed by fleshy berries, green at first, turning blue-black with a white bloom in the second year.

Uses: Oil from unripe berries used in massaging rheumatic or gouty parts of the body. Ripe berries are added as a flavoring to drinks such as gin, and meat dishes, especially game. Wood of stem and roots is burned to smoke preserved meats. **Caution:** use internally only under medical supervision; may also be an external irritant.

Cultivation: plant in autumn or spring in good, well drained soil in an open position. Propagate from seeds sown in a cold frame in spring, or from cuttings in autumn.

Parts used: leafy shoots at any time; fruit gathered in late summer and dried in sun; woody stems and roots when available.

Related species: *J. sabina* (savin): poisonous shrubby species used under supervision as a veterinary herb.

J. oxycedrus (prickly juniper): oil of cade (juniper tar) distilled from the roots as a veterinary vermifuge.

J. virginiana (eastern red cedar): source of cedar oil for perfume and medications.

Laurus nobilis (Lauraceae)
(Sweet) Bay (Tree)
sweet laurel, bay laurel

Description: large dense evergreen shrub or ornamental tree up to 50 ft, with glossy dark green, oval pointed leaves. Small creamy-yellow flowers appear in early summer, followed in warm climates and on mature plants by black berries.

Uses: an ancient aromatic and antiseptic plant, used to weave a victorious Roman general's crown or 'laurels'. Leaves are a popular culinary flavoring, and stimulate the appetite; when pulped they can be applied as an astringent to burns and bruises. Berries are pressed to make oil for liqueurs, perfume and veterinary uses.

Cultivation: grow in rich, well-drained soil in full sun, sheltered from cold winds; sometimes scorched or cut back by severe frost especially while young. Plant in early autumn or spring, and trim to shape in summer; may be clipped into formal topiary. Propagate by layering shoots in autumn, or from cuttings of side shoots in a shaded cold frame in early autumn. Best grown in containers and moved to a cool greenhouse in areas with severe winters.

Parts used: leaves at any time, dried in darkness and lightly pressed flat; ripe berries pressed for oil.

Related species: *Umbellularia californica* (Californian laurel): similar shrub or tree, with more aromatic foliage.

Lavandula angustifolia, syn. *L. officinalis, L. spica* (Labiatae)
(English) Lavender
true lavender

Description: evergreen perennial woody shrub, dense and branching up to 3 ft. Long narrow, aromatic leaves, gray-green and downy, and intensely fragrant blue-mauve flowers in long spikes in midsummer. A wild plant of Mediterranean hillsides; numerous varieties widely cultivated as garden ornamentals and hedging.

Uses: an early strewing herb, often burnt on low fires to perfume rooms. As an essential oil and in infusion used as a cough suppressant, and to treat headaches and nervous disorders. As an embrocation an external stimulant and antiseptic. Flowers attract bees, and are gathered for perfume, pot-pourri and to scent clothing.

Lavandula 'Hidcote'

Cultivation: grow in light, dryish soils in full sun for maximum fragrance and color. Sow seeds in trays in late spring; take soft cuttings in spring or hardwood cuttings in late summer; or layer old plants by mounding soil
(Continued)

**Lavandula
'Nana Alba'**

**English
lavender**

French lavender

Levisticum officinale, syn.
Ligusticum levisticum
(Umbelliferae)

Lovage
love parsley, lovage angelica, smallage

Description: pungent, clump-forming herbaceous perennial with rhizomatous roots and stout hollow ridged stems up to 8 ft. Broad glossy leaves, with large, dense umbels of greenish-yellow flowers in summer, followed by ridged golden-brown seedpods.

Uses: leaves can flavor soups and casseroles; stems are blanched like celery or candied like angelica; roots may be peeled and cooked as a vegetable; savory seeds are added to bread and other baked foods. Powdered root sometimes used as a condiment. Medicinally digestive and carminative. Essence of lovage used in perfumes. **Caution:** avoid taking large quantities.

Cultivation: mature plants are large and bulky, and so need plenty of room in deep rich moist soil, preferably in shade. Sow in spring outdoors in a seedbed or under glass, or divide roots in autumn or spring. Cut back once or twice during summer if a continuous supply of young leaves is needed.

Parts used: young leaves, avoiding the central flower stem; hollow main stems before flowering; roots of 2- or 3-year-old plants dug in autumn, sliced and dried; ripe seeds.

around the stems. Prune annually to shape in spring to prevent straggly growth and bare stems, especially on hedges, but do avoid cutting back into old wood.

Parts used: flowers gathered just before fully opened and dried slowly; flowering shoots and leaves distilled for essential oil.

Related species: L. a 'Hidcote': slow-growing species, with low stems and deep purple flowers.

L. a. 'Nana Alba': pale flowers; a low-growing species.

L. stoechas (French lavender): slightly tender species, with a stronger scent than most.

Related species: Ligusticum scoticum (Scots lovage): smaller wild plant of cliffs and seashores with milder flavor.

Levisticum chinensis: used in Chinese medicine for menstrual disorders.

Ligustrum vulgare (Oleaceae)
(Common) Privet
wild privet

Description: densely branched deciduous shrub up to 12 ft, with smooth leathery oval pointed leaves and short spikes of white strong-smelling flowers in early summer, followed by small black or yellow shiny berries. Grows wild in scrubland and open woods, especially on chalk, and often cultivated as a hedging plant; numerous attractive garden forms.

Uses: valuable hardwood timber for tools and charcoal; leaves once used by Shakers to make a mouthwash. Yellow dye made from the leaves. **Caution:** all parts are poisonous if ingested.

Cultivation: tolerant of most soils and positions. Sow seeds in autumn outdoors; put cuttings of young shoots in a cold frame in summer, or hardwood cuttings in a shady position outdoors in autumn. Plant and prune to shape in autumn.

Parts used: leaves at any time during the growing season; wood of larger pruned stems.

common privet

oval-leaved golden privet

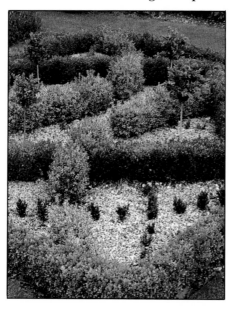

Related species: *L. ibota* (ibota privet): small elegant shrub, grown in China where insect damage to the stems produces a wax with industrial uses.

L. japonicum (Japanese privet, wax-leaved privet): dense, large-flowered species, with seeds sometimes roasted as a coffee substitute.

L. lucidum (wax tree): handsome small Chinese tree, seeds made into an infusion for strengthening general metabolism.

L. ovalifolium (oval-leaved privet): best species for hedging, dense and semi-evergreen, with popular golden variety.

Linaria vulgaris (Scrophulariaceae)
(Common) Toadflax
yellow toadflax, butter and eggs

Description: herbaceous perennial with vigorous underground creeping rhizomes and numerous long slender grayish flax-like leaves. Stems up to 2 ft bear in summer and autumn dense spikes of long-spurred brilliant yellow flowers like those of antirrhinums, each with a bright orange spot on the lower lip, followed by capsules of numerous flat round black seeds. A wild plant growing on bare waste ground.

Uses: a highly ornamental plant, used in the Middle Ages for laundry starch. Used homeopathically to treat diarrhoea and cystitis, and by herbalists to treat jaundice. Has a folk reputation as a fly poison when boiled in milk. Flowers yield dyes: yellow, orange, green or brown depending on the mordant used.

Cultivation: best grown in the wild herb garden, in a confined space, or in mown grass to restrain the invasive stolons. Sow in spring or early autumn, either where plants are to flower or in trays of compost for transplanting; established roots may be divided in autumn or spring. Plant 2 ft apart in full sun. Plants self-seed liberally, so dead-head after flowering to restrain seeding.

Parts used: whole flowering herb, fresh or dried in shade.

Linum usitatissimum (Linaceae)
🌿 **Flax**
flaxseed, linseed

Description: slender annual with wiry stems to 3 ft. Linear pointed leaves; pale to bright blue flowers (best for fiber production) or white in summer, followed by pods of flat oval brown seeds, rich in oil. Grows wild in dry grasslands, usually as an escape from cultivation. A taller variety is grown for flax production in cool, moist regions, and a more compact type in warm climates for seed.

Uses: stem varieties are soaked ('retted') in water to release fibers for making linen cloth. Linseed oil from seed varieties is one of the most important commercial drying oils, used in paints, varnishes and putty. Oil used medicinally as a laxative and vermifuge; the seeds soaked overnight and strained can be used to treat gastritis, constipation and indigestion, and in poultices for cuts, bruises and other abrasions. **Caution:** large doses may be poisonous.

Cultivation: sow in late spring or early summer in dry, well-drained soil in sun.

Parts used: whole fresh flowering plant for medicinal purposes; stems of green plant for fiber; seeds used fresh or dried and powdered.

Related species: L. catharticum (purging flax): white-flowered annual with oval leaves; used homeopathically to treat bronchitis and piles.

Lippia citriodora, syn. *Aloysia triphylla* (Verbenaceae)
🌿 **Lemon Verbena**
sweet-scented verbena, herb luisa, Spanish thyme

Description: perennial evergreen shrub, almost small tree up to 10 ft in warm climates, with sparse, slender branches and long narrow pointed leaves, gray-green and downy in groups of 3 or 4 with oil-bearing glands forming dots on the underside, giving off a penetrating lemon scent. Long terminal racemes of tiny white or lavender flowers in late summer.

Uses: tea (sold in France as 'verveine') made from leaves is tonic, calming and sedative, and can be used to treat nausea, palpitations and flatulence. Essential oil ('Spanish verbena') distilled from leaves used as flavoring in cakes, drinks, stuffings and desserts, in pot-pourri, and formerly in perfumes – largely replaced by lemon-grass oil. Hot leaf pulp is effective against toothache. **Caution:** large doses or prolonged use can cause internal irritation.

Cultivation: grow in fertile, well-drained soil in full sun, under glass in temperate regions as plants are frost-shy; in warm gardens may be trained as a climber against a sunny wall. Sow seed under glass in early spring, or take cuttings in summer. Propagate every few years, as older plants become threadbare and more sensitive to cold.

Parts used: leaves any time, fresh or dried in shade; shoots picked just before flowering and distilled for essential oil.

Lonicera periclymenum (Caprifoliaceae)
🌿 **(Wild) Honeysuckle**
woodbine

Description: deciduous woody twining shrub or climber to 20 ft, with oval glossy leaves. Clusters of fragrant pink-cream flowers appear in summer, followed by bright red berries.

Uses: as perfume, and a traditional remedy for a number of ailments. Bruised leaves used to treat skin disorders; flaked and infused bark for rheumatism and painful joints; flowers raw or infused in a tea for asthma and as a heart tonic; inside of the root as a veterinary vermifuge. Today only external uses are recommended. **Caution:** the berries of all honeysuckles may be poisonous.

Cultivation: grow in any good soil, in sun or shade, and train up walls or as standards on pillars. Sow seeds in autumn in pots (germination may be slow) or take cuttings in summer. Prune and mulch with compost in spring.

Parts used: leaves and flowers fresh or dried in shade; fresh bark from prunings; roots dug in autumn and dried.

Related species: L. caprifolium (perfoliate honeysuckle): yellow-flowered species with orange berries, used as an expectorant and antiseptic.

L. japonica: rampant semi-evergreen climber, an invasive weed in USA; widely used in Chinese medicine.

L. nigra (black honeysuckle): hard-wooded shrub with orange flowers, and black berries used homeopathically to treat neuroses.

Lythrum salicaria (Lythraceae)
🌿 Purple Loosestrife

Description: herbaceous perennial with creeping rhizomes and square angled stems up to 5 ft. Narrow, pointed leaves without stalks, in opposite pairs or whorls of three, and long, dense spikes of bright mauve-pink flowers in midsummer, followed by ovoid seed capsules. A plant of river banks and damp places, with several cultivated garden forms.

Uses: high tannin content, so once often used in leather tanning, but now a mainly decorative and medicinal plant. Antibacterial, used as a gargle and eyewash.

Cultivation: sow on surface of pots of moist compost and stand in trays of water until seedlings emerge; divide mature plants in spring or take cuttings in summer in a moist cold frame. Plant in damp soil in light shade, or full sun where the plants will flower best. Be careful that it does not choke out native plants when naturalized.

Parts used: flowering herb, fresh or dried in shade.

Malva sylvestris (Malvaceae)
🌿 Common Mallow

Description: coarse herbaceous biennial, sprawling or bushy to 3 ft. Leaves hairy, crinkled and deeply veined, palmate but almost circular at base of plant and toothed with long stalks, sometimes marked with a distinct black spot. Flowers pink, white or mauve with purple veins, in pairs or groups, in summer and autumn, followed by flat green button-like seed capsules. A wild plant of banks and waste places, especially near the sea, but also cultivated as a flowering plant in gardens.

pink mallow

Uses: whole plant is mucilaginous and therefore soothing. Leaves used to reduce inflammations and ease bee stings, and in poultices to treat ulcers and hemorrhoids. Tea made from an infusion of the flowers given for colds and bronchitis. Leaves can be added to soups or cooked like spinach, seedpods eaten raw or boiled. **Caution:** large amounts may be purgative and cause indigestion.

Cultivation: grow in full sun in well-drained ordinary soil. Sow in spring or autumn where plants are to grow, and thin seedlings to 2 ft. Older plants have a tendency to develop severe rust, and will need to be sprayed with fungicide or replaced regularly with young stock.

Parts used: flowers repeatedly over the long season, picked when fully open and dried fast in warmth; young leaves

white mallow

used fresh, or the entire plant cut down at flowering time and dried; seedpods picked while still green.

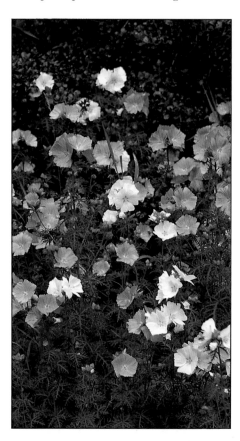

Related species: *M. neglecta* (dwarf mallow): almost prostrate bushy annual with pink or white flowers; similarly used, especially by North American Indians.

M. parviflora (least mallow, little mallow): short annual with pale pink flowers and similar culinary uses.

Matricaria recutita, syn. *M. chamomilla, Chamomilla recutita* (Compositae)

Wild Chamomile

scented mayweed, German chamomile

Description: aromatic annual with branched stems up to 18 in. Sweetly fragrant small white daisies with prominent yellow flowers with central hollow cones appear in early summer. A wild plant found in fields and roadsides, and a cereal 'weed' on chalky soils.

Uses: popular herb with a wide range of applications. Chamomile tea is refreshing, digestive and mildly sedative. Flowers reduce inflammation; used to soothe teething pains and poultice wounds. Essential oil used to scent shampoos and soaps. **Caution:** may cause a severe reaction in those with ragweed allergies.

Cultivation: sow in autumn or spring where plants are to flower, and water seeds in gently (do not cover). Grow in dry, chalky soils in full sun. Plants self-seed freely and may spread weedily unless checked.

Parts used: flowers, fresh or dried in shade.

Melilotus officinalis (Leguminosae)

(Common or Ribbed) Melilot

yellow sweet clover

Description: trailing or upright biennial with sturdy taproot and branched stems up to 4 ft. Leaves trefoil with long, toothed leaflets; flowers creamy-yellow and sweet-scented in loose stalked spikes in summer, followed by brown oval, wrinkled seedpods. Grows wild in pastures and bare waste places, and widely cultivated as a fodder and green manure crop.

Uses: the tea is tonic and anti-colic, used to treat sleeplessness, nervous tension, thrombosis and digestive disorders. Externally, often added to relaxing baths and made into a compress for slow-healing wounds. Both flowers and seeds are used for flavoring. **Caution:** excessive consumption may cause vomiting and dizziness.

Cultivation: sow seeds in late spring where plants are to grow, in fertile well-drained soils in full sun.

Parts used: leaves and shoots of flowering plants, fresh or dried in shade.

Related species: *M. alba* (white melilot, white sweet clover): taller plant with fragrant white flowers; widely grown as a fodder crop ('Bokhara clover') and bee plant.

Melissa officinalis (Labiatae)

(Lemon) Balm

bee balm, melissa, sweet balm

Description: hairy clump-forming herbaceous perennial with creeping roots and erect square stems up to 3 ft. Lemon-scented leaves, heart-shaped, toothed and deeply veined; flowers white or pale pink, sparsely arranged in a loose terminal spike in late summer. A wild plant of waste and derelict ground, widely grown in gardens, especially in golden and variegated forms.

Uses: vigorous and indestructible herb with a strong lemon fragrance. Young leaves used to flavor teas, soups, milk, custard, sauces, and added to liqueurs; pungent oil extracted from them is used in perfumery. Medicinally, balm lowers blood pressure, and is used in infusion to treat colds and influenza, nervous tension, insomnia, indigestion and other stomach ailments. A notable bee plant. Leaves and stems are sometimes used to polish and scent wooden furniture.

Cultivation: grow in rich, moist soil in full sun or light shade. Readily self-sows, or sow seeds in spring *in situ* or in trays under glass, or divide mature plants (advisable every 4-5 years to keep plants young and vigorous). Cut back in summer before flowering to encourage a further supply of young leaves.

Parts used: leaves and tips picked just before or after flowering, and used fresh or dried quickly in the shade (freezing retains more volatile oils than drying).

Mentha (Labiatae)

There are at least 18 species of mint and many more hybrids, most of them difficult to classify because of their variability and readiness to hybridize between each other. All are aromatic perennials, most containing menthol (essential mint oil) to some degree. **Caution:** handling mints may cause skin rashes and other allergic irritations; mint teas should not be drunk in large amounts over a long period.

Mentha x *piperita*
🍃 Peppermint

Description: hairy perennial with underground stolons and square pink or red stems up to 3 ft. Red-tinted oval, pointed leaves, deeply toothed and long-stalked, with mauve or white flowers on long spikes in midsummer. A hybrid between water mint and spearmint or corn mint (*M. arvensis*), found wild as an escape in hedgerows and rich moist soils; widely cultivated in gardens, and commercially for the essential oil.

Uses: the most medicinally valuable of all mints, with great cooling properties due to its high content of menthol. Used to treat gastric and digestive disorders, and nervous complaints such as tension and insomnia. Essential oil used to flavor confectionery, liqueurs and pharmaceutical products, and to scent cosmetics.

Cultivation: divide roots in autumn or spring, and plant in moist, fertile soil, cool in summer and with plenty of potash; cut back in summer to rejuvenate growth. Remake beds every 4-5 years, sooner if plants develop rust; or cultivate as an annual by containing the roots and replanting divisions every spring.

Parts used: leaves and stems, fresh or dried – gather before flowering for culinary use, in full flower for distillation of oil.

Mentha pulegium
🍃 Pennyroyal
pudding grass

Description: downy, bushy perennial with surface runners, and prostrate or erect stems up to 8 in. Small oval dark green leaves, hairy and slightly serrated, and mauve flowers in dense whorls in late summer. Grows wild on moist, light soils.

Uses: a very pungent herb, once used to disguise the flavor of putrid meat and still included in a few local dishes. Valued since Roman times as a flea repellent; also popular today as an aromatic ground-cover plant. Used medicinally to treat gastric ailments, headaches, colds, bites and minor abrasions.

Cultivation: sow in spring under glass, or divide plants in autumn or spring, and plant in light free-draining soil as edging or ground cover, or in the joints of paving stones.

Parts used: whole green plant, used fresh or dried.

pennyroyal

peppermint

Mentha x *rotundifolia*
🍃 Round-leaved Mint
apple mint

Description: sweetly aromatic perennial with shallow runners and slender, branched stems up to 3 ft. Oval, serrated leaves, soft green but paler and downy underneath, and slim spikes of white or pink flowers in late summer. Found wild as an escape on damp waste ground, and commonly grown in kitchen gardens, often in variegated or improved forms such as 'Bowles' Variety'.

Uses: the main culinary mint species in continental Europe, used to flavor both savory and sweet dishes, sauces and drinks.

Cultivation: as for *M.* x *piperita*.

Parts used: fresh leaves as required; can also be frozen or dried.

round-leaved mint

spearmint

Mentha spicata

❧ **Spearmint**
garden mint

Description: branching perennial with underground runners and square stems up to 30 in. Short-stalked leaves are oval and sharply pointed, deeply veined and serrated, either smooth and bright green or sometimes grayish, downy and wrinkled. Slim pointed spikes of mauve flowers appear in late summer. Found wild in moist shade on waste ground.

Uses: the least pungent species, subtly fragrant; one of the main culinary mints, yielding an essential oil used for flavoring confectionery, and dental and pharmaceutical preparations.

Cultivation: as for *M.* x *piperita.*

Parts used: fresh, frozen or dried leaves.

Related species: *M. arvensis* (corn mint): coarse wild species, sometimes gathered for culinary flavoring.

M. arvensis var. *piperascens* (Japanese mint): cultivated widely in the Far East as the main commercial source of menthol.

M. x *gentilis* 'Variegata' (ginger mint): popular compact ornamental variety with gold variegation.

M. x *piperata* var. *citrata* (eau de Cologne mint, bergamot mint): highly aromatic form with predominantly citrus fragrance, used to perfume cosmetics.

M. requienii (Corsican mint): prostrate tiny-leaved species; occurs wild, cultivated as ground cover; peppermint fragrance used in preparation of crème de menthe.

M. x *smithiana*, syn. *M. rubra raripila* (rust-free mint): purplish leaves and stems, spearmint flavor; least prone to mint rust.

M. suaveolens, 'Variegata' (pineapple mint): a variegated species with a distinct fragrance. Often grown as a decorative border herb.

ginger mint

pineapple mint

eau de Cologne mint

Monarda didyma (Labiatae)

❧ **Bergamot**
bee balm, Oswego tea, horsemint

Description: robust aromatic perennial with mat-like roots and runners that are sometimes invasive, and square stems up to 3 ft. Rough oval, serrated leaves, dark green or red-tinted, and large whorled heads of tubular red flowers in late summer, attractive to bees. Found wild, occasionally as an escape, in moist shaded woodland and on the banks of streams; more colorful but less fragrant varieties grown for ornament in gardens.

Uses: traditionally used to make a relaxing anti-depressant tea which can also be used to treat nausea and flatulence. An infusion is inhaled for colds, or used as an antiseptic for ulcers, wounds and acne. Included in potpourri mixtures and as a perfume in cosmetics. **Caution:** bergamot may cause photosensitivity in some people.

Cultivation: prefers rich moist light soil in sun or partial shade, mulched in dry seasons. Sow in spring, or divide mature plants every 2-3 years in spring.

Parts used: leaves and flowers, fresh or dried.

Related species: *M. fistulosa* (wild bergamot, purple bergamot): North American Indian tea and medicinal plant with purple (occasionally white or pink) flowers and a preference for drier soils.

Myrica gale (Myricaceae)
🐝 Bog Myrtle
sweet gale, sweet willow

Description: deciduous shrub with shiny reddish, upright twiggy stems to 4 ft, and long narrow, gray-green leaves. Dense, yellow-brown catkins in spring are followed by orange, waxy berries. A rare wild plant of wet heaths, bogs and moorland.

Uses: tonic tea made from leaves, which are sometimes used with berries for flavoring cooked dishes and treating dysentery; dried leaves used as moth and flea repellent. Roots and bark give yellow dye.

Cultivation: grow in damp acid soils in shade, and prune in winter. Propagate in autumn from seeds sown outdoors, or from cuttings, layers or division.

Parts used: leaves, fresh or dried, or distilled for essential oil; berries fresh or dried; roots and bark.

Related species: *M. carolinensis* (bayberry): bushy shrub up to 8 ft, found on dry sandy soils; blue-gray waxy berries, used for candles.

M. cerifera (wax myrtle, candleberry): large shrub up to 30 ft; root bark used as circulatory stimulant and to treat diarrhoea; wax from berries made into candles.

M. rubra: oriental species, cultivated for edible seeds.

Myrrhis odorata (Umbelliferae)
🐝 (European) Sweet Cicely
myrrh

Description: bushy herbaceous perennial with a thick taproot and stout hollow grooved stems branching to 5 ft. Hairy, sweetly scented bright green leaves, soft, thin and ferny; loose umbels of small white flowers in early summer, followed by dark brown seeds, ridged and sharp-tipped. Grows wild in hedgerows and grassy shade on high ground, and cultivated locally.

Uses: leaves and unripe seeds are eaten raw in salads, roots and leaves boiled as vegetables. One or two leaves at a time are included in conserves and tart fruit dishes to add sweetness and aniseed flavor; also added to brandy and liqueurs. Whole plant is tonic and gently laxative, and used in healing ointments. Dried seeds ground as a spice in Germany; leaves used to polish and scent oak furniture; horses are sometimes lured with a piece of the root.

Cultivation: divide roots in spring or autumn, or sow seeds in autumn in trays outside or where plants are to grow (frost is needed for germination). Transplant while young to deep, rich, shady soil in a moist location; plants self-seed freely and may be invasive in heavy soils.

Parts used: leaves fresh or dried, seeds, green and immature, or dried; roots dug in autumn; whole green plant for medicinal infusions.

Myrtus communis (Myrtaceae)
🐝 Myrtle

Description: evergreen shrub, slow-growing in cool climates to 10 ft, stems with flaking red-brown bark. Long oval, leaves, dark green, shiny and dotted with oil glands. Scented flowers, white or rose-pink in late summer, followed by dark purple berries (some varieties white). Grows wild on Mediterranean scrubland and seashores.

Uses: The perfume *eau d'ange* is distilled from flowers and leaves to scent soaps and cosmetics; leaves added as flavoring to meat dishes; fruits fermented into alcoholic drinks. Medicinally, crushed leaves applied to external wounds, rashes and skin irritations; juice of berries good for stomach and digestive ailments. Dried buds and fruits used as a peppery condiment; roots and bark for tanning leather.

Cultivation: plants prefer fertile well-drained, acid soils, in full sun with good light; in cool regions the added warmth of a sunny wall is beneficial, or plants may be grown in large pots under glass. Prune to shape after flowering; dense foliage can be clipped into simple topiary. Propagate from cuttings under glass in summer, or seeds sown in greenhouse in spring.

Parts used: leaves fresh or dried; flower buds dried; flowers fully open; fruits fresh or dried; roots and bark.

Related species: *M. ugni*, syn. *Eugenia ugni*, *Ugni olinae* (Chilean guava, murtillo): small shrub with fragrant rose-pink flowers, and mahogany-red fruits used in jams and preserves.

Nasturtium officinale, syn.
Rorippa nasturtium-aquaticum
(Cruciferae)
❧ **Watercress**

Description: lush aquatic or marginal
perennial, almost evergreen, spreading by hollow brittle fleshy stems that
root at each leaf joint. Leaves dark
green and silky, oval or pinnate, older
leaves burnished bronze. Racemes of
small white flowers in summer followed by short, fat pods containing
two rows of seeds (only one in some
species). Grows wild in ditches and
streams and widely cultivated in flood-
ed beds as a salad herb in two main
varieties: green or summer, and frost-
hardy brown or winter cress.

Uses: leaves, rich in minerals and vita-
mins C and A, prized since Roman
times for biting, rich flavor, raw or
cooked as a vegetable and in soups.
Also used as a cough remedy. Crushed
leaves are applied as poultice for
rheumatism and gout; raw seeds used
as vermifuge. **Caution:** do not con-
sume excessive quantities, and gather
wild plants only from clean running
water; plants in stagnant and polluted
water may be host to the dangerous
liver fluke.

Cultivation: sow in a moist, shady border in spring; divide plants, or root
pieces of stem in pans immersed in
water in spring. Plant in beds irrigated
with flowing water, in tubs of soil and
water, or in trenches of fertile moist
soil. Water frequently.

Parts used: older leafy stems, fresh or
dried; seeds when ripe.

Related species: Rorippa palustris (yellow cress): Australian wild herb with
crinkled leaves and yellow flowers.

Nepeta cataria (Labiatae)
❧ **Catmint**

catnip, catnep

Description: pungent, hairy perennial
growing in a dense leafy mound. Long
branching leafy stems up to 3 ft bear
light gray, heart-shaped leaves, coarse-
ly serrated and almost white beneath;
and from summer to autumn persis-
tent flowers, white with mauve markings, in whorls. Grows wild in open
spaces and roadsides on moist chalky
soils, and commonly cultivated in gardens.

Uses: well known for its popularity with
cats – volatile oil is a feline aphrodisiac
and also distilled for perfumes. Leaves
made into a mint-flavored tea for
colds, nervous tension, flatulence and
gastric disorders, or poultices for cuts
and bruises.

Cultivation: divide roots in spring or
autumn, or take cuttings in summer,
and grow in light, well-drained soil in
full sun. Also easily grown from seed.
Cut back after flowering.

Parts used: leaves and flowering stems,
fresh or dried in shade.

Nicotiana alata, syn. *N. affinis*
(Solanaceae)
❧ **Flowering
Tobacco**

sweet-scented tobacco

Description: tropical perennial, usually
grown as ornamental annual, with
fleshy roots and strong, simple stems
up to 6 ft. Long, tubular flowers, highly fragrant and white or pink, are followed by capsules of small seeds.
Numerous cultivated strains, some
dwarf, in various colors.

Uses: occasionally used as stimulant
for nervous system, but normally
grown as a handsome flowering plant
in herb gardens.

Cultivation: sow under glass in spring,
or outdoors in frost-free areas, and
transplant to flowering positions in
full sun. Water frequently in dry
weather.

*Related species: N. bigelovii, N. attentu-
ata, N. benthamiana* and numerous
other wild species have been used
by indigenous peoples in North
America and Australia as snuff and
ritual smoking tobacco.

N. rustica (nicotine tobacco) and *N.
tabaccum* (common tobacco) are
the main cultivated forms for commercial production of smoking
tobacco, nicotine insecticide and
citric acid.

Ocimum basilicum (Labiatae)

🌿 (Sweet) Basil

St Joseph wort

Description: bushy aromatic annual with brittle branched stems to 2 ft. Leaves oval, shiny, fleshy and fragile, dark green or red tinted, such as dark opal basil; flowers creamy white or mauve in whorls, in midsummer. Grows wild in hot, humid regions, and cultivated extensively in numerous forms such as Greek, lemon, red or ruffled basils.

Uses: popular culinary flavoring, typical of Mediterranean cuisines and used since ancient times (remains have been found in Egyptian burial chambers). Oil of basil used in perfumery, soaps, cosmetics and liqueurs. Plant is claimed to be an insect repellant, and can be used medicinally to soothe pain and treat vomiting, nervous stress and headaches.

Cultivation: sow under glass in spring or outside after risks of frost are past. Grow in rich, moist soil, with full sun and shelter from cold winds; or treat as a pot plant, sowing in small pots to avoid root disturbance. Pinch out flowering shoots to extend useful life of plants, and root non-flowering side shoots in pots during summer for winter use.

Parts used: leaves fresh or frozen, or dried in shade (flavor will change considerably).

Related species: *O. kilimandsharicum* (camphor basil): African hairy perennial used to treat coughs and colds.

O. minimum (bush basil): hardier small-leaved dwarf plant, 6 in, uses as for sweet basil; flavor bitter-resinous.

O. sanctum, syn. *O. tenuifolium* (holy basil): large, hairy plant with pink flowers; sacred in India, where it is known as *tulsi.*

O. viride (fever basil): West African species, used as a tea to treat fevers.

sweet basil

dark opal basil

purple ruffled basil

bush basil

Oenothera biennis (Onagraceae)

🌿 (Common) Evening Primrose

evening star, king's cure-all

Description: coarse biennial herb with thick fleshy taproot, and overwintering rosette of long, narrow willow-like leaves, bright green and wavy-edged with a reddish midrib. Robust flower stems to 6 ft bear large, sweet-scented pale yellow trumpets with red sepals in summer, individual blooms lasting only a single day, followed by elongated seed capsules. Grows wild in dry, sandy places; occasionally cultivated as a crop.

Uses: leaves are a winter pot herb, and may also be used to treat coughs and chest ailments. North American Indians have many uses for the plant, especially the roots, used in poultices for piles and boils; roots, sometimes known as German rampion, also eaten raw or cooked; ripe seeds used in bakery like poppy seeds. Medicinally the plant is an important source of gamma-linoleic acid, with other uses still under test.

Cultivation: sow in summer where plants are to grow, or in a seedbed for transplanting in autumn. Grow in full sun in light, well-drained soil.

Parts used: leaves, shoots and flowers for fresh culinary use; roots dug in autumn or early the following spring before growth resumes.

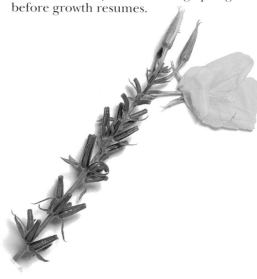

Related species: *O. erythrosepala* (large-flowered evening primrose): larger flowers with red stems, and edible shoots and roots.

Olea europaea (Oleaceae)
🐝 **Olive**

Description: slow-growing evergreen tree with gnarled trunk and slender gray, fissured branches, to 30 ft. Leaves dark green, scaly and gray beneath, narrow oblong or pointed. White, fragrant flowers in panicles in summer are followed by hard ovoid fruits, green at first but later purple-black, with a single hard stone. Thorny wild form grows on stony hillsides in Mediterranean regions, cultivated forms widely grown in groves.

Uses: since ancient times the principal source of edible oil in the eastern Mediterranean area; biblical symbol of peace. An olive wreath was given to victors in the Olympic Games. Not only the fruits but also the leaves are edible. Oil pressed from the fruits is a major culinary and medicinal product, sometimes used as a laxative and in enemas, and in treatments for minor wounds.

Cultivation: trees only grow well away from frost and tropical heat. Grow in dry, well-drained warm soils, with winter protection in cool regions, or in large pots under glass. Prune where necessary in spring. Propagate from seeds sown in warmth in autumn, or from cuttings taken in summer and rooted under glass.

Parts used: leaves; fruits picked when green, pink or red, or fully ripe, sometimes cracked, fermented and soaked in brine, or pressed for oil.

Origanum vulgare (Labiatae)
🐝 **Oregano**
wild marjoram, joy of the mountain, Mexican sage

Description: bushy, spicily aromatic perennial with horizontal woody rootstock and stems, often reddish, to 30 in. Downy gray-green leaves, oval pointed and toothed, and small tubular flowers in clusters, pink or mauve with darker bracts, in late summer. Found wild on dry, fertile hillsides, usually on chalk, and widely grown both as a crop and a garden plant, often in variegated forms.

Uses: tonic, digestive and expectorant herb, used to treat coughs and sore throats, indigestion and gastric upsets. Antiseptic leaves are chewed for toothache, and added to baths and poultices. Important culinary flavoring for meat dishes and salads, the leaves are also made into tea and beer, or distilled into an oil for perfumes and cosmetics.

Cultivation: sow in spring outdoors and thin or transplant to 12 in apart, or divide mature clumps in spring. Plant in light, well-drained soil in full sun (flavor more pungent in warmth), or grow in pots or a greenhouse border in cool regions.

Parts used: sprigs of leaves and flowers, or whole clump cut almost to ground

oregano

pot marjoram

level when in flower, for use fresh or dried in shade.

Related species: *O. dictamnus* (dittany of Crete): gray-leaved perennial with large, pink flowers; leaves have oregano flavor, used medicinally since Minoan times as painkiller and wound healer. *O. prismaticum* and *O. heracleoticum* (winter marjoram) have similar flavor, especially effective when dried.

O. majorana (sweet marjoram, knotted marjoram): sun-loving tender perennial often raised from seed each spring as an annual; mainly European culinary herb, with same medicinal uses as oregano.

O. onites (pot marjoram): tender perennial with white or pink flowers, for cooler gardens; ornamental plant also used like sweet marjoram.

Osmunda regalis (Osmundaceae)
🌿 **Royal Fern**
buckthorn brake

Description: dense, clump-forming perennial terrestrial fern, with heavy rootstock of tangled, matted fibrous roots, and elegant buff-pink fronds up to 6 ft, streaked with creamy yellow in spring, later vivid green and turning golden brown in autumn. Leaflets at tips of fronds have spore-bearing sori in late summer. Grows wild in wet shady meadows.

Uses: handsome ornamental fern with mucilaginous roots, often boiled in water to produce royal fern jelly, once given to invalids as a nutritious, easily digested food, and also used to treat dysentery, coughs and pulmonary disorders. Dried roots (osmunda fiber) are a traditional ingredient of orchid potting composts.

Cultivation: grow in rich, moist soil, in damp shade or semi-shade. Mulch with compost every spring; water freely in dry weather. Divide in autumn or spring, or sow spores on surface of moist compost under glass in spring.

Parts used: main roots, fresh or dried, for medicinal use; thinner fibrous roots dried for compost.

Pelargonium graveolens
(Geraniaceae)
🌿 **Rose Geranium**

Description: tender perennial, green and succulent at first but later woody with light brown bark, growing up to 4 ft. Flowers small and pale pink in dense umbels in summer and autumn. Commercially grown for oil distillation; popular house plant in temperate regions.

Uses: rose-scented leaves used to scent desserts, cakes and teas, pot-pourri, drinks and fingerbowls. Oil distilled from the leaves is an insect repellent, used in perfumes.

Cultivation: sow seeds indoors in spring, or take cuttings in late summer and plant out the following summer in dry soils and full sun. Often grown as a house plant, best stood outdoors in summer to keep compact. May be grown permanently outdoors in warmer regions, cutting plants down in autumn and mulching with leaves or straw where light frost is possible.

Parts used: leaves, fresh or dried; all green parts, cut just before flowering for oil distillation.

Related species: *P. capitatum*, *P. radens*: alternative sources of rose-geranium fragrance. Other common species include *P. crispum* and *P. citriodorum* (lemon), *P. fragrans* (nutmeg), *P. nervosum* (lime), *P. odoratissimum* (apple), *P. parviflorum* (coconut), *P. tomentosum* (peppermint).

Petroselinum crispum
(Umbelliferae)
🌿 **(Wild) Parsley**

Description: biennial or short-lived perennial with rosette of rich green leaflets (tightly curled in many cultivated forms). In early summer a glossy, solid sharp-edged leafy flower stem, up to 30 in, bears flat-topped umbels of yellow-green flowers, followed by capsules of brown seeds. Cultivated in gardens in numerous forms such as curly, plain 'Italian' and turnip-rooted Hamburg parsley.

Uses: tea made from leaves or roots used to treat jaundice, coughs and menstrual problems, rheumatism, kidney stones and urinary infections; juice expressed from them soothes conjunctivitis and eye inflammations. Both seeds and dried roots are used as spices; seeds, which contain poisonous apiol, are sometimes infused to produce an external vermifuge. **Caution:** avoid parsley during pregnancy or if suffering from kidney inflammation.

Cultivation: sow in spring in trays or outdoors in rich, moist soil – soak seeds for 24 hours in warm water or pour boiling water into seed drills immediately before sowing, as fluctuating temperatures hasten germination. Sow again in midsummer for winter use or for pots indoors.

Italian or continental parsley

curly-leaved parsley

Parts used: leaves, fresh, frozen or dried; roots dug in winter and dried; seeds when capsules are ripe.

Phlomis fruticosa (Labiatae)
Jerusalem Sage

Plantago major (Plantaginaceae)
Greater Plantain
broadleaf plantain, rat's tail plantain, waybread, white man's footprint

Description: tough-rooted perennial with coarse basal rosette of long-stalked, elliptical leaves, pointed and deeply veined. Tall, dense cylindrical spikes of tiny greenish-yellow flowers appear in summer, up to 18 in, followed by a spike of seeds enclosed in sticky gelatinous pods. Found wild in cultivated land, waste ground, lawns and footpaths, where the spread of its sticky seeds is helped by passers-by. A local field crop in France, and also cultivated in gardens in improved forms.

Uses: an old herb, one of the nine sacred Saxon species and recovered from remains of Iron Age Tollund Man. The crushed leaves are cooling and pain-relieving, used in poultices and ointments for wounds and abrasions; an infusion of leaves or boiled roots is a useful gargle and eyewash; fresh leaves may be taken for both constipation and diarrhoea, according to the dosage. Very young leaves may be cooked like spinach; seeds are popular in Chinese and Malaysian drinks, and complete seedheads are fed to caged birds.

Cultivation: wild variety rarely grown deliberately, but seeds may be sown *in situ*, barely covered, in moist, fertile light soil or loam, in spring or autumn. Plants self-seed freely.

Parts used: leaves, fresh or dried quickly in sun or shade; roots, dug in winter and boiled; seed spikes, gathered in bags when they turn brown, and rubbed to free the seeds.

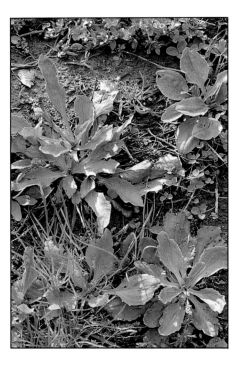

Related species: P. *coronopus* (crowfoot plantain, buckshorn plantain): biennial with dandelion-like leaves, used in salads while very young.

P. *lanceolata* (ribwort plantain): perennial with long, narrow leaves and short dense ribbed stem of yellow-brown flowers, used as cough remedy and wound healer.

P. *media* (hoary plantain): decorative perennial with scented, pink and white fluffy flowers, a great favourite with bees.

P. *ovata* (ispaghula): annual with medicinal seeds, producing a laxative and emollient oil.

P. *psyllium* (fleaseed), P. *indica* (branched plantain): annuals with branching globular heads of greenish flowers; known in Latin America as *llanten*, used in same way as ispaghula.

Description: aromatic evergreen shrub with stout branching stems up to 10 ft. Silvery-green, wedge-shaped leaves are wrinkled and densely covered with yellow woolly hairs. Clear or rusty yellow tubular flowers appear in whorls in late summer. Grows wild in arid Mediterranean and Asian regions, and commonly grown as a shrub in herb and mixed borders.

Uses: mainly a handsome ornamental shrub; leaves sometimes made into an aromatic sage-flavored tea, especially in Greece and neighbouring Mediterranean countries.

Cultivation: sow seeds in spring, take cuttings in summer or divide in spring or autumn. Grow in dryish, well-drained soil in full sun.

Parts used: leaves, fresh or dried in the sun.

Portulaca oleracea (Portulacaceae)

✏ **(Wild) Purslane**

pigweed

Description: warm-climate annual, with fleshy pinkish stems, prostrate and branching to 12 in, bearing fleshy spatulate leaves, green or red-tinged. Small yellow flowers appear in the leaf axils in late summer, followed by seed capsules with opening lids and filled with numerous tiny black seeds. Grows wild in dry soils in vineyards and on hillsides in warm regions, a common weed in Australia, New Zealand and the United States; cultivated as an edible crop in the form var. *sativa* (kitchen-garden purslane), a larger erect plant with fleshy green or gold leaves.

Uses: ancient vegetable crop in India and Iran, still used as a salad herb and cooked vegetable. Infusion of the green plant is cooling and soothing, taken for fevers, headaches and chest complaints, and applied to skin rashes and abrasions. Seeds are an Australian Aboriginal wild condiment.

Cultivation: sow mid-spring in light, well-drained soil; water and feed regularly. Sow again for succession at monthly intervals until late summer.

Parts used: fresh leaves and stems, preferably before flowering, cut just above ground level.

Poterium sanguisorba, syn. *Sanguisorba minor* (Rosaceae)

✏ **Salad Burnet**

Description: clump-forming perennial with strong woody rootstock, and red, furrowed stems branching to 2 ft. Gray-green pinnate leaves with rounded leaflets, each deeply indented, and small, bright red-brown petalless flowers in dense globular heads in early summer. Found wild in fields, woods and waste ground on dry chalk.

Uses: young leaves eaten as salad herb with cucumber-like flavor, and added to soups, sauces and cheeses. Leaves are digestive, and in infusions used to treat diarrhoea and haemorrhages. Decoction of root applied to cuts and burns; roots also produce a black dye and are used in tanning leather.

Cultivation: sow in spring in trays under glass, or divide roots in spring and plant in fertile soil in sun or light shade. Remove flowers to extend useful season for leaves. Plants self-seed very easily.

Parts used: young leaves before flowering; whole green plant, fresh or dried; roots dug in spring and dried.

Related species: P. officinale, syn. *Sanguisorba officinalis* (great burnet, bloodwort): taller herb with deep red, rectangular flowerheads; similar uses.

Prunella vulgaris (Labiatae)

✏ **Selfheal**

heal-all, woundwort, carpenter's herb

Description: downy perennial with creeping rhizome and square stems to 12 in. Long narrow oval leaves, bright green, pointed and toothed; flowers purple, pink or white in dense whorls in midsummer. Grows wild in moist meadows and pastures; many cultivated forms with larger flowers grown in gardens.

Uses: used in Middle Ages according to the 'Doctrine of Signatures' to treat throat conditions and internal bleeding, and regarded as a panacea by North American Indians and Chinese physicians, the latter using the seeds for nervous complaints. Flowering plant may be eaten in salads and cooked vegetable dishes, used to prepare a styptic for wounds, and made into gargles or mouthwashes for mouth ulcers and sore throats.

Cultivation: take cuttings or divide plants in spring, and plant out 8 in apart as ground cover in moist shade or full sun. In fertile soils plants are much larger than normal and may be invasive; growing in turf helps restrain unnatural growth.

Parts used: green flowering plant, fresh or dried in shade.

Pulmonaria officinalis
(Boraginaceae)
&. Lungwort
maple lungwort, spotted dog,
Jerusalem cowslip

Description: downy perennial with
creeping rootstock; stems hairy and
unbranched, up to 12 in. Rough
leaves in a rosette over winter, broadly
oval and pointed, green with gray
spots, stem leaves narrower. Flowers
bell-shaped in small, leafy sprays, pink
at first and later becoming blue, or
white or purple, in early spring. Grows
wild in woods and hedgerows on
chalk; often cultivated as ground
cover in shade.

Uses: ancient cure for lung disorders
according to 'Doctrine of Signatures'.
Young leaves used as spring pot herb
in soups, stews and salads; flowering
plant made into a tea for gastro-
intestinal and pulmonary ailments;
homeopathically used for bronchitis
and colds. Powdered roots and lower
leaves are wound-healing.

Cultivation: divide in autumn or after
flowering, and plant in light soils, not
too dry, in shade or semi-shade. Lift,
divide and replant every 4-5 years.

Parts used: young fresh leaves gathered; green flowering plant, fresh or
dried; roots dug in winter, cut, dried
and powdered.

Related species: *P. saccharata*
(Bethlehem sage): larger plant,
with leaves heavily marked with silver, flowers appear as lilac, white or
blue; grown as a foliage plant; similar uses to *P. officinalis.*

Reseda luteola (Resedaceae)
&. **Weld**
dyer's rocket

Description: coarse unbranched biennial with an overwintering rosette of
long, narrow wavy-edged leaves. In
summer stout leafy stem, 5 ft, termi-
nates in long, slim spike of small
bright yellow or yellow-green flowers.
Found growing wild in dry disturbed
soils in chalky areas.

Uses: traditional dye plant, once widely cultivated or gathered from the wild
for brilliant yellow or reddish-yellow
color extracted from leaves, flowers
and stems.

Cultivation: sow seeds where plants are
to flower, in late summer in well-
drained, fertile soil with a little lime.
Seedlings appear in spring and should
be thinned to 18 in apart.

Parts used: whole green plant gathered
at flowering time.

Related species: *R. lutea* (wild
mignonette): similar to weld, but
shorter with divided, wrinkled
leaves; popular and decorative bee
and butterfly plant.

R. odorata (common mignonette):
perennial normally grown as an
annual, both outdoors and in pots,
for its intensely fragrant tiny yellow
and white flowers, from which oil is
extracted for perfume; a soothing
herb for calming nerves, healing
wounds, and treating asthma and
hayfever; once used to stuff pillows
as a remedy for insomnia.

Rosmarinus officinalis (Labiatae)
&. **Rosemary**

Description: dense, woody evergreen
perennial, up to 10 ft. Bushy stems
with cracked gray bark and downy
young shoots are covered with narrow
aromatic, hard leaves, dark and shiny
above, grayish beneath. Short racemes
of small blue flowers appear in early
summer. Grows wild on dry, rocky
slopes and cliffs in warm regions, and
widely cultivated both commercially
and in gardens in numerous forms.

Uses: ancient strewing herb and
Romany charm, hung up to ward off
evil; popular culinary flavoring added
to meat dishes, baked foods and
Mediterranean recipes. Leaves medicinally valuable and for treating depression, migraine, and disorders of the
liver and digestion. Leaves also made
into ointment for neuralgia, rheumatism, eczema and minor wounds, and
used in hair rinses and mouthwashes.
Caution: excessive quantities or frequent use may cause poisoning.

Cultivation: sow seeds in trays in
spring, take cuttings in summer in a
cold frame, or layer plants in autumn.
Plant in well-drained, alkaline soil,
in a sunny position sheltered from
winds. Some forms are slightly tender
and may need protection in winter.

Parts used: leaves gathered at flowering time, used fresh or dried in shade.

Rubia tinctorum (Rubiaceae)

⚘ **Dyer's Madder**

dyer's cleavers

Description: herbaceous perennial with long fleshy complex yellow rootstock and red fibrous roots, and stiff square, prickly climbing stems up to 3 ft, with whorls of pale green bristly leaves, long and pointed. Clusters of small greenish-yellow flowers appear in midsummer, followed by blue-black berries. Grows wild in hedges and thickets on chalk, often as an escape from former wide cultivation.

Uses: infusions of leaves and stems treat constipation, and liver and bladder disorders; powdered root is wound-healing, often used for skin ulcers. Homeopathically used to treat anaemia and ailments of the spleen. Most popular use of the roots is as a variable red to purple dye.

Cultivation: sow seeds or divide plants in spring or autumn, and plant in deep well-broken, alkaline soil in full sun or semi-shade.

Parts used: leaves and stems; roots peeled and dried quickly, and powdered or fermented.

Related species: *R. peregrina* (wild madder): similar plant, though coarser in appearance, producing a paler red dye.

Rumex rugosus, syn. *R. acetosa* (Polygonaceae)

⚘ **Common Sorrel**

French sorrel

common sorrel

Description: leafy perennial with thin vertical rootstock, and basal clumps of thick shiny, arrow-shaped leaves. Leafy slender flower stems in early summer, slightly branching to 4 ft, bear loose spikes of small red-brown flowers. Grows wild in damp fields and waste land.

Uses: popular, sharply flavored pot herb since ancient Egyptian times, widely used by medieval apothecaries. Cooling and blood-cleansing, often taken as a spring tonic tea. Leaves made into poultices for acne and other skin complaints, and if picked very young can be eaten raw or cooked, notably in sorrel soup; juice of leaves will curdle milk and has also been used as a stain remover ('salts of sorrel'). Roots make a bitter tonic and a treatment for diarrhoea. **Caution:** leaves are high in oxalic acid and should be eaten sparingly; handling them may cause skin irritations.

Cultivation: sow in spring, thinning seedlings to 12 in apart, or divide roots in autumn. Grow in rich, moist soil, and keep well watered. Gather leaves frequently and remove flower stems to extend cropping.

Parts used: young leaves and buds, picked before flowering, and used fresh or frozen; roots fresh in summer.

Related species: *R. acetosella* (sheep sorrel, red sorrel): small smooth arrow-shaped leaves, piquant in salads or less sour cooked.

R. alpinus (monk's rhubarb): broad leaves, and thick creeping rhizome used in infusion as a treatment for constipation.

R. crispus (curled dock, yellow dock): tall with large, wavy leaves, used for skin complaints; root is laxative, powdered to make mouthwash and gargle; stems stewed like rhubarb; seeds ground and used in baking.

R. patientia (herb patience, sorrel-dock): tall and branched, leaves with low acidity, can be used as spinach substitute.

R. scutatus (French sorrel, round-leaved sorrel): short leafy plant, low in oxalic acid, used as a salad ingredient and pot herb.

R. vesicarius (ruby dock, wild hops): thick broad leaves and tall, bright red flowers; leaves popular vegetable with Bedu, young shoots can be added to salads.

Ruta graveolens (Rutaceae)

Rue

herb of grace

Description: semi-evergreen perennial shrub with woody base and branching stems up to 3 ft. Powerfully aromatic green or blue-green leaves divided into a number of spatulate leaflets, dotted with shiny oil glands. Loose racemes of small pungent yellow or yellowish-green flowers appear in summer. Found wild on dry, rocky limestone soils; cultivated in gardens as an ornamental shrub, often in blue, gold or variegated forms.

Uses: ancient medicinal herb, formerly used as an antidote to poisoning and a talisman against witchcraft. A favourite Arab herb, the only one to be blessed by Mohammed; leaves used homeopathically to treat phlebitis and varicose veins, and herbally for epilepsy, nervous complaints and uterine disorders. Essential oil used in perfumery and cosmetics; small amounts of the pungent foliage used for flavoring foods and alcoholic drinks. **Caution:** to be taken internally only under medical supervision, and used externally with care as allergic skin reactions are possible.

Cultivation: sow in a seedbed outdoors in spring, or take cuttings in late summer, and plant in full sun in well-drained soil with a little lime.

Parts used: leaves from flowering plant, fresh or dried in shade.

Salvia officinalis (Labiatae)

Sage

Description: variable evergreen perennial shrub, with strong taproot, and square woody, branching stems up to 2 ft 6 in, gray and woolly when young. Gray-green, pebbly-textured soft leaves are oblong or lanceolate, and finely toothed. Whorls of violet-blue flowers appear in spikes in summer. Found wild on hillsides and grassland on chalk in warm regions; widely cultivated as a pot herb in Mediterranean countries; popular herb garden shrub with numerous forms and decorative varieties, some gold or variegated. Best culinary sages are the plain narrow-leaved and non-flowering broad-leaved types.

Uses: an ancient herb, popular as a potent condiment for meat, fish, Mediterranean dishes, English Sage Derby cheese, and as a basis for sage tea, taken to counteract sweating. Infusion used to treat depression, nervous anxiety and liver disorders; homeopathic preparations given for circulation and menopausal problems. Leaves are also antiseptic, used in gargles for laryngitis and tonsillitis,

common sage

variegated sage

and as a mouth freshener and tooth cleanser. Essential oil used in perfumery.

Cultivation: grow in well-drained, rich soil, in full sun and with shelter from cold winds. Propagate from cuttings in spring and summer, or by layering (mounding for older bushes). Nip off points of shoots to induce bushy growth, and renew every 4-5 years as shrubs become leggy.

Parts used: leaves fresh, or dried in shade, picked before flowering for herbal use or when in flower for oil distillation.

clary sage

(Continued)

(Sage *continued)*

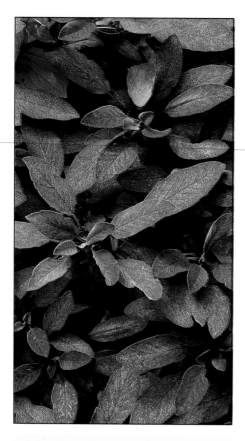

Related species: *S. azurea*: large blue-flowered perennial shrub, used in Mexico as a herbal panacea.

S. sclarea (clary sage): biennial with white, blue or pink flowers; leaves infused as a gargle and skin healer; source of muscatel oil for flavoring and perfumery.

S. viridis, syn. *S. horminum* (clary): annual, very similar to clary sage and similar uses; often grown as a flowering bedding plant.

S. horminoides (wild clary), *S. verbenaca*: purple-flowered species with jagged, toothed leaves and red stems; uses similar to clary sage.

S. fruticosa, syn. *S. triloba* (three-lobed sage): large perennial with lobed leaves, grown in Mediterranean countries for making the popular sage tea.

S. rutilans (pineapple sage): tender perennial with scarlet flowers in autumn and winter; fresh leaves add strong pineapple flavoring to desserts and drinks.

Sambucus nigra (Caprifoliaceae)

ᔒ **(Common) Elder (Berry)**

Description: deciduous shrub or small tree with roughly fissured bark and numerous straight branches, up to about 30 ft. Leaves pungent and dull green, with 5-7 elliptical leaflets; red flowering stems bear broad, flat-topped heads of small white, fragrant flowers in midsummer, followed by numerous edible purple-black berries. Found wild in hedgerows, woods and built-up areas; commercially cultivated on a local scale; ornamental varieties (white, gold, cut-leaf) frequently grown in gardens.

Uses: legendary tree, long held to be guardian over all other herbs, with numerous virtues according to the part used. Leaves are an effective insect repellent, and soothing in ointments for skin complaints. Flowers soothe the eyes, are added to cosmetics, make a calming tea, and are popular for their sweet fragrance in drinks and fruit dishes. Fruits are used in cordials, syrups and preserves; medicinally to induce sweating and to treat coughs, colds, catarrh and throat infections; and as a blue-purple dye. Bark is an old treatment for epilepsy, and (together with the leaves) is laxative; root used for kidney ailments.

Cultivation: usually harvested as a wild plant, but may be grown in almost any soil and position (variegated forms best positioned in full sun for maximum color). Propagate by hardwood cuttings, easily rooted outdoors in autumn, or by suckers.

Parts used: leaves, flowers and fruits, fresh or dried; root and bark gathered as needed.

Related species: *S. canadensis* (American elder): smaller North American species with similar appearance and uses.

S. ebulus (dwarf elder, danewort): dwarf, strong-smelling perennial with creeping rhizomes, otherwise similar to common elder; used homeopathically for dropsy; berries give a blue dye; bark and flowers purgative (berries dangerously so).

S. racemosa (red-berries elder): small tree with more pointed leaves, flowers in early dense clusters, and scarlet berries in summer; purgative oil extracted from the seeds.

Santolina chamaecyparissus, syn.
S. incana (Compositae)
🌿 Santolina
cotton lavender

Description: pungent evergreen perennial shrub with branched white stems up to 20 in, silver-gray filamentous leaves, toothed along the edges. Fragrant small, bright yellow flowers like hard round buttons appear in midsummer. Grows wild in dry rocky places and warm soils; popular in gardens as an ornamental shrub and dwarf hedging plant.

Uses: grown and used since classical Greek times as a vermifuge and moth repellent. Infusion of leaves used as a rub for rheumatism and painful joints; flowers make a tonic tea. Perhaps most popular today as a decorative hedging plant for parterres and knot gardens.

Cultivation: grow in well-drained, light soil in full sun. Propagate by layering, or root cuttings with a heel in autumn or spring outdoors or in a cold frame. Clip hedges to shape in spring, and again at flowering time if only foliage is important.

Parts used: leaves before flowering, dried and stripped from stalks; flowers.

Related species: S. neapolitana (Italian lavender): taller plant with very feathery gray foliage and pale lemon-yellow flowers; similar uses.

Satureja hortensis (Labiatae)
🌿 Summer Savory
bean herb

Description: hairy aromatic annual with tough straggly or erect stems, up to 18 in. Long, dark green leaves, leathery and pointed, and lilac-pink or white flowers in small spikes from the leaf axils in late summer. Grows wild in dry, light soils and on rocky hillsides on chalk; locally cultivated for commercial use; popular garden herb.

summer savory

Uses: culinary herb whose use dates back to the early Romans; potent flavoring enhances all others in the same way as salt. Used sparingly in meat dishes and stuffings, with peas, beans and cabbage to improve their digestibility, and liqueurs. Infusion of leaves treats gastric upsets, indigestion and loss of appetite; tea is tonic. Spreading flowering shoots between clothing repels moths.

Cultivation: sow seeds in spring where plants are to grow, in well-drained soil in full sun. Species is sensitive to cold: delay sowing until the worst frosts are past, or grow the hardier winter savory. Plants self-seed freely.

Parts used: leaves gathered before flowering, fresh or dried in shade; flowering shoots fresh or dried.

winter savory

Related species: S. montana (winter savory): semi-evergreen bushy and woody perennial shrub, with smaller pink or white flowers and a slightly stronger flavor; commercially cropped for essential oil; other uses similar.

Scabiosa arvensis, syn. *Knautia arvensis* (Dipsaceae)
🐾 Field Scabious
blue buttons, pincushion flower

Description: evergreen perennial, with short rootstock and creeping stolons, long indented leaves. Bristly stem, up to 3 ft, bears flat heads of mauve flowers in late summer, followed by densely hairy seedheads.

Uses: infusion of roots treats cuts, sores, abrasions and itching; whole herb used as a remedy for dandruff. Homeopathically used for eczema and skin disorders.

Cultivation: sow in trays in autumn or spring, divide roots in spring or take cuttings of short side shoots. Grow in full sun in fertile, well-drained soil.

Parts used: whole flowering herb including roots, fresh or dried; roots dug in autumn, fresh or dried.

Related species: Succisa pratensis, syn. *Scabiosa pratensis* (devil's bit, daisy fleabane): perennial with purple, blue or white flowers; root used for wounds and diarrhoea; leaves eaten raw or cooked like spinach.

Scutellaria galericulata (Labiatae)
🐾 (Common) Skullcap
helmet flower

Description: downy perennial with creeping rhizome; short-stalked oval pointed leaves, bluntly toothed and dark green, with red veins on underside. Stems, up to 12 in, in summer bear large slender tubular bright violet-blue flowers in pairs. Found wild in moist lowlands, especially wet meadows.

Uses: bitter tonic and digestive herb; powerful nerve tonic, used in infusion to treat depression, headaches, insomnia, irritability and similar disorders. (Out of flower, skullcap is easily confused with wood sage, *Teucrium scorodonia*.)

Cultivation: sow seeds outdoors in spring, or divide roots in spring, and grow in good moist soil in an open, sunny position.

Parts used: all green parts during flowering, fresh or dried.

Sedum acre (Crassulaceae)
🐾 Biting Stonecrop
wall pepper, golden-carpet, gold moss

Description: succulent mat-forming perennial shrub with sprawling stems, and erect branches up to 8 in crowded with overlapping cylindrical short green fleshy leaves, hot and peppery to the taste. Leafy stems extend in midsummer and produce bright yellow flowers, 5-petalled and star-shaped, in loose clusters. Grows wild on walls and roofs and in dry stony soils, often on lime; and in gardens as a wall, rock garden and edging plant.

Uses: plants were often grown deliberately on roofs as charms against lightning. Homeopathically used to treat piles; bruised leaves, fresh or in ointments, are soothing for wounds, abcesses, bruises and minor burns. **Caution:** slightly poisonous; internal use may cause dizziness and nausea.

Cultivation: grow in full sun in dryish, sandy soil with a little lime. Sow seeds outdoors or divide roots in spring, or scatter some of the cylindrical leaves which root freely where they fall.

Parts used: leaves, fresh or dried in warmth.

Related species: S. reflexum (reflexed stonecrop): long-stemmed robust perennial, with long cylindrical leaves and golden-yellow 7-petalled flowers. Fresh non-flowering shoots are often added to soups and salads, or cooked as a tangy vegetable.

Sempervivum tectorum
(Crassulaceae)

Houseleek

hen-and-chickens

Description: fleshy perennial with short-stemmed rosette of tightly packed fleshy gray-green leaves, sometimes red-tipped, arranged in a spiral. Stem elongates in summer to form a thick leafy flower stem, 8 in high, with clusters of small rose-pink star-like blooms. Grows wild on walls, roofs and rocky mountain sites; often cultivated in pots, sinks and rock gardens.

Uses: ancient magical herb, planted on roofs as an insurance against fire and lightning. Sliced or crushed leaves used to poultice stings, burns, rashes and itching skin, and to cure warts and corns. Sometimes used as a skin lotion. In some parts of Europe young leaves and shoots are eaten as a vegetable.

Cultivation: grow in full sun in crevices and mortar joints packed with a little ordinary soil, or in sinks and pots filled with gritty compost. Propagate from seeds or leaves in trays at any time.

Parts used: leaves, sliced or pulped, as needed.

Silybum marianum (Compositae)

Milk Thistle

variegated thistle, Our Lady's milk thistle, spotted thistle

Description: prickly annual or biennial, with a thick taproot and downy white, furrowed stems up to 4 ft. Leaves oblong, wavy and spiny-edged, glossy dark green with clear white veins, and flowers red-purple and thistle-like above a collar of spiny bracts in mid-summer.

Uses: the herb has had a reputation for treating liver disorders since classical Roman times, and is included in several proprietary medicines for this purpose. Used in herbal infusions and homeopathic preparations for liver and abdominal ailments. Young shoots and leaves are edible and an Arab delicacy; roots may be cooked like parsnips, and base of flowerheads in the same way as artichokes; stems can be peeled and boiled as a vegetable; seedlings eaten raw in salads.

Cultivation: sow in spring in a sunny bed where plants are to grow, and thin seedlings to 2 ft apart.

Parts used: seedlings; young leaves and shoots; flower stems just before flowering; roots after flowering; flowerheads for medicinal use, fresh or dried in thin layers in warmth.

Smyrnium olusatrum
(Umbelliferae)

Alexanders

black lovage, horse parsley

Description: pungent biennial with solid ridged stems up to 5 ft, and large shiny, dark green leaves divided into several trefoil toothed leaflets. Flowers yellow-green and glistening with nectar, in small round umbels in midsummer, followed by globular capsules of aromatic black seeds. Grows wild on rocky banks and sea cliffs.

Uses: bitter herb cultivated since early Greek times; root is diuretic, seeds a condiment, crushed leaves or their juice a soothing and healing treatment for cuts and minor abrasions. Grown as a salad and pot herb before celery became popular, with the leaves, stems, shoots and flower buds all used, sometimes after blanching, in soups and fish dishes.

Cultivation: grow in full sun in moist soil. Sow in spring and grow as an annual leaf crop, or in autumn to overwinter and produce larger stems the following year.

Parts used: young leaves; young stems, after blanching with soil or straw if preferred; roots fresh or dried; ripe seeds.

Solidago virgaurea (Compositae)
🐿 **Golden Rod**

Description: herbaceous perennial with a stout knotted rhizome, and downy slender leafy stems occasionally branched, up to 5 ft. Leaves narow oval or lanceolate, and toothed; flowers tiny, bright yellow and powdery, in panicles on branched spikes in late summer. Found wild in woods, hedges and the edges of fields; commonly grown as an ornamental plant in several cultivated forms.

Uses: a medieval Arab healing herb, also used by North American Indians; made into poultices for external wounds, and infusions for fevers and digestive upsets. Occurs in several proprietary medicines for kidney and bladder ailments, and used homeopathically to treat these, as well as arthritis and rheumatism.

Cultivation: sow in spring outdoors, or divide in autumn or spring, and grow in light soils in full sun or light shade. Lift, divide and replant every 3-4 years.

Parts used: green flowering plant before flowerheads fully opened, fresh or dried in shade.

Stellaria media
🐿 **Common Chickweed**

Description: variable fast-growing clump-forming or sprawling annual, with weak branching straggling stems, up to 18 in long, each with a single line of longitudinal hairs. Small soft, oval fleshy leaves, long-stalked and yellowish-green, and tiny white flowers with separate thin petals, at any time. A common 'weed', forming dense mats on moist, cultivated and waste ground.

Uses: an ancient pot herb; seeds found in Neolithic burial sites. Traditionally fed to domesticated birds and fowls; a bitter salad and pot herb; homeopathic remedy for rheumatism. Poultice of stems and leaves used to ease arthritis and pains of the joints, cuts, skin irritations and inflammation.

Cultivation: seldom necessary. Plants self-seed themselves all too freely in all soils and positions, especially in dry weather.

Parts used: young stems and leaves, fresh or dried.

Symphytum officinale (Boraginaceae)
🐿 **Comfrey**
knitbone

Description: stout rough perennial with thick brown, fleshy rootstock, and clumps of upright basal hairy leaves, long, oval and pointed. Branched stems up to 4 ft bear purple, pink or white bell-shaped flowers in forked, curled clusters in summer. Found wild in streams, ditches and other wet places; widely cultivated in selected forms for garden use.

Uses: root formerly a popular internal remedy for gastric disorders and a homeopathic treatment for ulcers. Leaves used in infusion for bronchitis, and in poultices for wounds, bruises and eczema. Young leaves and shoots were eaten as a vegetable, cooked with a change of water. Older leaves commonly used after wilting as an animal feed, for making compost and liquid fertilizer, and for mulching plants. **Caution:** absolutely not to be used internally under any circumstances – recent evidence suggests the plant is carcinogenic.

comfrey

Cultivation: divide roots in spring or autumn, or take root cuttings in spring. Plant in moist soil in sun or shade, and mulch annually with decayed manure for maximum leaf production. Lift, divide and replant every 3-4 years. May need containment.

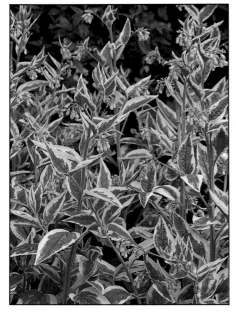

Russian comfrey

variegated
Russian
comfrey

Parts used: leaves, fresh, wilted or dried; roots fresh or split lengthways and dried in sun.

Related species: *S.* x *uplandicum* (Russian comfrey): stiffly hairy, vigorous hybrid with larger leaves, cultivated for leaf production (up to 4-6 cuts per year); often found wild in dry places as an escape.

Tanacetum parthenium, syn.
Chrysanthemum parthenium,
Matricaria parthenium
(Compositae)

Feverfew

Description: robust downy perennial with branched stems up to 3 ft. Leaves yellow-green and pungent, divided into several smaller rounded leaflets. Flowers small white daisies with prominent yellow centers, in dense clusters in midsummer.

Uses: a bitter-flavored herb, long used as a tonic and to treat indigestion, but currently popular as a treatment for migraine. Leaves are made into pain-soothing poultices for limb and joint aches, and whole flowering stems are an insect repellant, keeping moths away from clothing. A popular bee plant. **Caution:** not to be taken during pregnancy; fresh leaves may cause mouth ulcers.

Cultivation: sow in spring outdoors on the surface and water in, or take cuttings in summer. Grow in dry, well-drained soil in full sun. Plants self-seed very easily.

Parts used: leaves or whole green flowering plant, fresh or dried in shade.

Related species: *T. vulgare,* syn. *Chrysanthemum vulgare* (tansy): pungent perennial, with feathery dark green leaves and flat heads of yellow button-like flowers; an old strewing herb, insect repellent (companion plant to ward off aphids) and vermifuge; crushed leaves used to treat bruises and varicose veins; leaves once added to lamb dishes and spring puddings.

Taraxacum officinale agg.
(Compositae)

Dandelion

blowball

Description: complex group of perennials with long, stout taproots, and milky sap. Flowers on hollow stems, often reddish and downy near the top, up to 18 in; large, sweet-scented and yellow, in late spring to early autumn, followed by fluffy heads of numerous seeds, each with a parasol of white hairs to aid wind distribution.

Uses: leaves are a diuretic; dried to make tonic teas; added to herbal beer; blanched for salads. Flowers used in wines, schnapps, pancakes and in Arab baking; inside surface of flower stems soothes burns and stings (also stains skin). Roots roasted as a coffee substitute, cooked in Japanese cuisines, and give a magenta dye (with the leaves they produce brown dyes). Medicinally, given for gall-bladder and liver complaints.

Cultivation: often gathered from the wild, but may be grown as an annual by sowing in full sun in spring, barely covering seeds.

Parts used: leaves fresh or dried in warmth; flowers when fully opened in sun; roots dug in summer for medicinal use, or autumn for drying and grinding for coffee.

Related species: *T. kok-saghyz* (Russian dandelion): similar Russian wild plant, with rich milky sap, producing latex, used together with roots of *Scorzonera tau-saghyz* to make rubber.

Microseris scapigera (Australian dandelion): similar plant with larger flowers and stout yam-like root used as a vegetable by Aborigines.

Teucrium chamaedrys (Labiatae)
🐌 **Wall Germander**

Description: semi-evergreen perennial with purplish stems, sprawling or upright to 12 in. Leaves oval with rounded teeth; flowers dark lilac-purple, pink or white, in summer.

Uses: leaves used in tonic teas, wines and liqueurs, and for treating digestive and gall-bladder disorders. Plants used for edging and hedges in herb and knot gardens.

Cultivation: sow seeds in spring outdoors, take cuttings in summer, or divide plants in autumn. Grow in well-drained soil with a little lime. Clip hedges in spring and again in mid-summer.

Parts used: whole flowering plant, fresh or dried in shade.

Related species: *T. fruticans* (tall germander): larger plant with white stems, blue-green leaves and large blue flowers.

T. scorodonia (wood sage, wood germander): pebbly sage-like leaves and yellow flowers, smelling faintly of garlic, prefers acid soils in shade; leaves used to heal and dry wounds, and in teas inhaled for throat and sinus problems.

Thlaspi arvense (Cruciferae)
🐌 **Field Pennycress**

Description: strong-smelling annual with branched stem to 18 in, oval leaves, often clasping the stem. Small white flowers in spikes appear in spring and summer, followed by pods containing black seeds. Grows wild in waste places, and sometimes a troublesome 'weed' of arable ground.

Uses: finely chopped leaves have a spicy flavor like watercress, and are used in salads and cooked dishes. Seeds were once ground and used as a mustard.

Cultivated: rarely necessary, but may be sown *in situ* in spring in fertile soil.

Parts used: leaves and young shoots before flowering; seeds dried in the sun and ground.

Related species: *T. alliaceum* (garlic pennycress): similar plant, with earlier flowers, narrow seedpods and scent of garlic, similar uses.

Thymus vulgaris (Labiatae)
🐌 **Common Thyme**
garden thyme

Description: variable aromatic perennial evergreen shrub with gnarled thin, square stems, woody at the base, prostrate or upright to 12 in. Leaves small, elliptical and gray-green, paler beneath; small flowers in summer, lilac or white, fragrant and popular with bees. Found wild on warm, dry rocky banks and heaths; widely grown commercially for the leaves and essential oil; favourite culinary and hedging herb in gardens, with numerous decorative and variegated forms.

Uses: popular since classical times, thyme has a number of important uses. Leaves make a tonic and stimulating tea, used to treat digestive complaints and respiratory disorders, especially for loosening mucus. Antiseptic and vermifuge essential oil (thymol) added to disinfectants, toothpaste, perfumes, toiletries and liqueurs. A culinary herb with a powerful flavor, thyme is added sparingly to bouquets garnis, stuffings and savory dishes.

common thyme

Cultivation: sow seeds or take cuttings in summer; divide plants in spring, or layer older bushes by mounding. Plant in very well drained soil in full sun. Clip after flowering and again in autumn; replace every 4-5 years, and in cold climates protect in winter, grow in containers or as a hedge.

lemon thyme

caraway thyme

wild thyme

Parts used: leaves and flowering tips, fresh or dried in sun.

Related species: T. capitatus (cone-head thyme): large-flowered species, grown commercially for essential oil production.

T. x *citriodora* (lemon thyme): light green species with pink flowers and strong lemon scent.

T. herba-barona (caraway thyme): arching stems rooting at tips, bronze-green leaves, strong caraway flavor.

T. mastichinus: gray-green leaves and pink flowers; widely grown in Spain for flavoring, marinades and as essential accompaniment to olives.

T. serpyllum (wild thyme, mother of thyme): very hardy, mat-forming species with late red-purple flowers and mild flavor; ideal for herb lawns; reputation as a herb for women's ailments.

Trifolium pratense (Leguminosae)
🌿 Red Clover

Description: short-lived perennial often grown as an annual, with branching roots, and arching stems, up to 20 in. Leaves long-stemmed and trefoil. Flowers pink-mauve in summer and autumn.

Uses: dried flowers produce a volatile oil and a soothing tea for promoting sleep; taken medicinally as an expectorant for respiratory disorders, and to treat skin problems such as eczema and psoriasis. Externally, an infusion soothes burns and sores. Flowers also make a good wine and yield a yellow dye.

Cultivation: sow in spring (rub the seeds with sandpaper to improve germination) in free-draining, slightly alkaline soil in rows or patches.

Parts used: flowerheads, fresh or dried in shade.

Related species: T. alexandrinum (berseem, Egyptian clover): very tall white fodder crop grown in Egypt and Middle East.

T. amabile (Aztec clover): Mexican and South American species, eaten as a pot herb mixed with cereals.

T. hybridum (alsike clover): small white-flowered hybrid grown as fodder and green manure in cold regions and on wet acid soils.

T. repens (white clover, Dutch clover): creeping, drought-resistant perennial with larger leaves and fragrant white or pinkish flowers liked by bees; numerous cultivated forms.

Tropaeolum majus (Tropaeolaceae)
🌿 Nasturtium

Description: South American perennial grown in temperate climates as an annual, with creeping or climbing stems to 10 ft. Leaves bright green or blue-green. Flowers orange, sometimes red or yellow, in summer and autumn, followed by spherical fruits, first green and then brown, containing three large seeds.

Uses: antiseptic and digestive herb, also used to treat respiratory and urinary disorders; seeds are a vermifuge, and crushed for use in poultices for boils and sores. Leaves are edible and used in salads, the flowers as a garnish, and both seeds and flower buds are pickled for their pungent mustard-like flavor.

Cultivation: sow spring or early summer where plants are to grow, or in pots for transplanting after frosts cease. Grow in full sun with shelter from wind, in rich soil for leaf crops, poorer dry ground for flowers and seeds.

Parts used: leaves fresh or dried; flowers; seeds while green, or when ripe for grinding as seasoning.

Tussilago farfara (Compositae)

ᔒ Coltsfoot

coughwort, horse-hoof

Description: robust herbaceous perennial with white, scaly creeping stolons, and pale red downy, scaly stems, up to 12 in, bearing golden-yellow dandelion-like flowers that open in sun in early spring. Sturdy long-stemmed fragrant leaves follow in late spring from basal clumps, rounded or heart-shaped, irregularly toothed and up to 12 in in diameter, pale beneath with a network of clear veins. A wild plant of ditches, moist banks, waste places and loamy soils.

Uses: leaves are an important cough remedy for bronchitis and laryngitis, commonly added to herbal smoking mixtures. Both leaves (after crushing the veins) and flowers can be used in poultices for sores and ulcers; root is boiled to make coltsfoot rock or candy. Flowers are made into wine, and mature leaves can be dried and burnt to an ash used as a salt substitute. **Caution:** roots contain similar substances to comfrey, and may be equally dangerous if taken internally.

Cultivation: usually gathered from the wild, but seeds may be sown in moist soil in summer, or plants divided in autumn or used for root cuttings in winter. Plant where exposed to sunlight for most of the day. In some soils may become invasive.

Parts used: flowers before fully open, fresh or dried in shade; leaves in summer, fresh or cut up and dried in shade.

Urtica dioica (Urticaceae)

ᔒ Stinging Nettle

Description: stinging perennial with branching roots, and bristly stems sprawling or erect up to 6 ft. Leaves covered in stinging hairs; tiny yellow-green flowers, females hanging like catkins, males in spikes in summer and autumn.

Uses: young shoots and leaves widely used in spring soups and as a green vegetable, and added to beer. Older leaves laxative in infusion, expectorant and styptic. Made into hair restorers and used homeopathically to treat skin ailments. Stems fibers are strong enough for linen weaving, papermaking and spining into ropes. Foliage is a commercial source of chlorophyll and an effective compost activator. **Caution:** handle with care, as the formic acid injected by serious stings may cause recurrent 'nettle rash'.

Cultivation: rarely necessary, but seeds may be sown in summer in fertile soil, or roots can be divided in spring.

Parts used: leaves gathered before flowering, fresh or dried in sun.

Related species: U. breweri, U. thunbergiana: North American and Japanese species respectively.

U. urens (annual nettle, burning nettle): smaller plant with reddish stems and small oval deep green leaves; similar uses.

Valeriana officinalis (Valerianaceae)

ᔒ Valerian

garden heliotrope, cat's valerian

Description: deciduous perennial with strong-smelling branching roots, and stout tubular furrowed stems, up to 4 ft. Leaves bright green and pinnate, with 2-10 pairs of shiny oval leaflets, pointed and toothed. Small white or pink flowers in branching terminal clusters in summer. Grows wild in ditches, woods and fertile grassland.

Uses: mildly sedative and antispasmodic, used to treat tension, anxiety, insomnia, migraine and nervous ailments, as well as colic and cramp; externally in infusion for eye problems. Attractive to cats. An occasional culinary flavoring. **Caution:** large doses or extended use may lead to addiction.

Cultivation: sow in spring where plants are to grow, or separate stolons in autumn and plant in moist borders or beside pools. Tolerates full sun or deep shade; plants benefit from an annual dressing of manure.

Parts used: roots at least 2 years old and gathered after leaves fall, used fresh or dried in shade.

Related species: V. celtica (nard, spike): prostrate plant with brownish-yellow flowers, grown in rock gardens.

V. edulis: North American species with large tapering roots, occasionally cooked as a root vegetable.

V. phu (Cretan spikenard): white-flowered species with ornamental golden garden form; similar uses.

Veratrum viride (Liliaceae)
🌿 Green False Hellebore

American white hellebore, itchweed, Indian poke

Description: statuesque clump-forming perennial with strong, thick roots, rosette of broad elliptical pleated or ribbed leaves. Hairy, robust stems up to 5 ft bear branched spikes of pale green or greenish-white 6-petalled star-like flowers in summer. A wild plant of moist grassy places on hills and mountain pastures (not to be confused with *Helleborus viridis*, green hellebore).

Uses: handsome flowering plant for a prominent position, anti-parasitic; used by North American Indians as an arrow poison, and by the pharmaceutical industry in preparations for reducing blood pressure. **Caution:** highly toxic and not for home preparation.

Cultivation: divide roots in autumn or spring, or sow seeds in trays of peaty soil in a cool greenhouse in spring (seeds take several months to germinate). Grow in moist semi-shade.

Parts used: roots dug in autumn, cut in pieces and dried in sun or warmth.

Related species: *V. album* (white hellebore, langwort, false helleborine): similar plant with yellowish-green flowers with similar uses; roots dried and ground into 'hellebore powder', an insecticide.

Verbena officinalis (Verbenaceae)
🌿 Vervain

Description: hairy branching perennial with woody rootstock, and slender rough angular stems up to 3 ft, bearing long sparse 3-lobed leaves, dull grayish-green and toothed. Small lilac flowers in thin stiff spikes in late summer. Found wild in hedges, waysides and dry barren places; commonly cultivated in France and other European countries.

Uses: ancient herb popular with druids as a panacea, and used in the Middle Ages to ward off plague. Used homeopathically for dropsy; medicinally to treat rheumatism, and stomach and liver disorders. Tea is a stimulant, and relieves fevers and nervous tension. Externally used for sores and skin problems, and for eye complaints.

Cultivation: sow in spring or autumn on the surface of well-drained soil in full sun; lightly press or water in the seeds and thin seedlings to 12 in apart.

Parts used: green flowering plant, fresh or dried in sun or warmth.

Veronica officinalis (Scrophulariaceae)
🌿 (Heath) Speedwell

fluellen

Description: hairy prostrate mat-forming perennial, with stems creeping and rooting at nodes or erect to 12 in. Small rough leaves in opposite pairs, oval and finely toothed; flowering shoots from leaf axils, in summer bearing bright lilac-blue flowers with a white eye, in clusters. Grows wild in pastures and woods, and on dry slopes and heaths on acid soils.

Uses: a medieval healing herb, still used in a tonic tea ('Swiss tea') for liver, digestive and general intestinal complaints. Fresh juice used for skin ailments, for which there is also a homeopathic preparation. Cultivated as an ornamental ground-cover plant in the garden.

Cultivation: sow in spring or divide plants in early summer, and grow in rich, fertile soil in full sun. Water freely in dry weather, and replace plants every 4-5 years.

Parts used: whole green flowering plant, fresh or dried in shade or a warm room.

Related species: *V. beccabunga* (brooklime, water pimpernel): fleshy aquatic perennial with small, bright blue flowers found beside streams and in other wet places; popular salad plant high in vitamin C, and a very mild purgative.

Veronicastrum virginicum, syn. *Veronica virginica* (culver's root, bowman's root): very tall slender blue- or white-flowered perennial, once used by Shakers as a digestive. **Caution:** highly purgative.

Vinca minor (Apocynaceae)
Lesser Periwinkle

Description: evergreen perennial, with stems prostrate and rooting at leaf nodes, and leafy flowering stems erect to 2 ft. Leaves glossy and oval, flowers pale blue with lighter centers, or white, on hollow stalks in early summer.

Uses: used as a gargle for sore throats, as a styptic and astringent for wounds, sores and ulcers, and in a tea to reduce blood pressure and hypertension. **Caution:** large amounts may be toxic, leading to circulatory disorders.

Cultivation: divide in spring or take stem cuttings in autumn, and grow in fertile moist soils with a little lime.

Parts used: green flowering plant in spring, fresh or dried.

Related species: *Vinca major* (greater periwinkle, blue buttons): longer-stalked leaves and stems rooting only at the tips.

Viola tricolor (Violaceae)
Wild Pansy

heartsease, field pansy, johnny jump-up

Description: variable annual or short-lived perennial, almost evergreen, with hollow stems sprawling or erect to 8 in. Leaves oval and indented. Flowers yellow with purple and white markings, from spring to autumn, followed by capsules filled with shiny, light brown seeds, splitting into three segments when ripe.

Uses: renowned mild heart tonic, used to treat high blood pressure, indigestion and colds; cleanses blood and induces perspiration. Also used to treat dropsy and rheumatic conditions, and for skin disorders such as acne and eczema.

Cultivation: sow spring or summer where plants are to grow; press seeds into soil but leave uncovered. Surplus seedlings may be transplanted to any position in semi-shade. Plants self-seed freely. Cut back leggy plants to induce bushy growth and further flowers.

Parts used: green flowering herb and root, fresh or dried in shade.

Related species: *V. odorata* (sweet violet): trailing stoloniferous perennial with sweet-scented purple, white or pink flowers; ancient strewing herb and commercial crop for perfume industry; leaves and flowers used to treat coughs, catarrh and respiratory disorders; flowers crystallized.

V. sororia, syn. *V. papilionacea*: North American purple-flowered wild species with several cultivated forms; used by Indians for colds and headaches.

Vitex agnus-castus (Verbenaceae)
Chaste Berry

Indian spice, monk's pepper, chaste tree

Description: aromatic shrub or small tree up to 20 ft, with palmate leaves divided into narrow leaflets on gray, downy shoots. Small violet fragrant flowers in dense trusses growing up to 12 in long in autumn, followed in warm climates by purple-black berries. Found wild on light, stony soils in southern Europe; cultivated as a garden ornamental, sometimes with white flowers.

Uses: an ancient Greek herb thought to guarantee chastity, now used to regulate female hormonal activity. Also reputed to be a male anaphrodisiac; used as symbolic strewing herb in Italian monasteries. Seeds are used as a peppery condiment, slender branches in basketwork.

Cultivation: sow seeds in spring, layer in summer, or take cuttings under glass in autumn. Grow in well-drained, light soil, in full sun, and against a warm sheltered wall in temperate regions.

Parts used: fruits picked in autumn, fresh or dried in shade.

Related species: *Vitex negundo* (Chinese chaste tree): medium shrub with square stems and lavender flowers in late summer.

Right: *A fruitful, healthy herb garden – the results of only a little research and planning.*

BEE AND BUTTERFLY HERBS

- anise
- betony
- chicory
- comfrey
- evening primrose
- hyssop
- lemon balm
- mint
- sage
- thyme
- yarrow

- bergamot
- broom
- chives
- coltsfoot
- fennel
- lavender
- meadowsweet
- rosemary
- self-heal
- valerian

AN ESSENTIAL HERB COLLECTION

- basil – a tender annual
- bay – grown as a small trained specimen
- chives – for edging
- dill – an annual
- fennel – bulky and tall
- French tarragon – tall, best in a container
- lemon balm – a herbaceous perennial
- marjoram – shrubby

- mint – best in a pot
- parsley – ideal for edging
- rosemary – a bushy shrub
- sweet cicely – American (*Osmorrhiza longistylis*) or European (*Myrrhis odorata*)
- thyme – mats of evergreen foliage
- winter savory – short evergreen shrub

HERBS FOR FIRST AID

Part of the herb garden can be reserved for a selection of plants to provide help in emergencies; most can be used fresh in teas, compresses and infusions.

- aloe vera – grow as a pot plant and use a broken leaf to relieve sunburn
- lavender – use as an infusion for coughs, colds and headaches
- pot marigold – make a poultice from the flowers for burns and stings
- witch hazel – use in compresses for bruises and bleeding

- German chamomile – can be taken as a tea for insomnia
- lemon balm – infuse for digestive and menstrual upsets
- St John's wort – use as a compress for cuts and small wounds

PLANTS FOR FORMAL OUTDOOR TOPIARY

- box
- cephalotaxus
- *Cupressus sempervirens*
- holly
- *Ligustrum japonicum*
- *Thuja occidentalis*
- cassinia
- *Cryptomeria japonica*
- *Eugenia myrtifolia*
- ivy – on a wire frame
- *Phillyrea angustifolia*
- yew

PLANTS FOR A GRAY AND WHITE HERB BORDER

- *Acorus calamus* 'Variegatus'
- *Artemisia* 'Powis Castle'
- *Buxus sempervirens* 'Elegantissima'
- *Chrysanthemum balsamita*
- *Iris pallida* 'Variegata Argentea'
- *Mentha suaveolens* 'Variegata'
- *Nepeta cataria*
- *Ruta graveolens* 'Variegata'
- *Sambucus nigra* 'Albovariegata'
- *Thymus* 'Silver Posy'
- *Althaea officinalis*
- *Artemisia absinthium* 'Lambrook Silver'
- *Chamaemelum nobile* 'Flore Pleno'
- *Colchicum autumnale* 'Alboplenum'
- *Marrubium vulgare*
- *Myrtus communis* 'Variegata'
- *Primula vulgaris* 'Alba Plena'
- *Salvia sclarea*
- *Symphytum* x *uplandicum* 'Variegatum'
- *Vinca major* 'Variegata'

MARY FLOWERS

These are just a few of the numerous plants suitable for inclusion in a traditional St Mary Garden.

- *Alchemilla mollis*, lady's mantle
- *Cardamine pratensis*, lady's smock
- *Galium verum*, lady's bedstraw
- *Primula veris*, cowslip (Our Lady's keys)
- *Tanacetum balsamita*, costmary
- *Calendula officinalis*, marigold
- *Convallaria majalis*, lily of the valley (Our Lady's tears)
- *Lilium candidum*, Madonna lily
- *Silybum marianum*, Our Lady's milk thistle

Add to these any flowers that are white (for purity) and blue (the color of the Virgin Mary's robe), together with the monastic strewing herbs hyssop, tansy and meadowsweet as symbols of purity.

Index

Stockists and Suppliers

HERB SEEDS AND PLANTS

Cameron Park Botanicals
Highway 64 East
Raleigh, NC 27610
(Newsletter; catalogue available)

Caprilands Herb Farm
Silver Street
North Coventry. CT 06238

Flag Fork Herb Farm
260 Flag Fork Road
Frankfurt, KY 40601
(Catalog available)

The HerbFarm
32804 Issaquah-Fall City Road
Fall City, IA 98024
(206) 784 2222
(Catalog: $3.50)

Richter s Herb Catalogue
Goodwood
Ontario,
Canada, LOC 1A0
(416) 640 6677
(Catalog: $2.00 US and Canadian)

Seeds Blum
Idaho City Stage
Boise, ID 83706
Fax (208) 338 5658
(Catalog: $3.00)

Taylor s Herb Gardens
1535 Lone Oak Road
Vista, CA 92084
(691) 727 3485
(Catalog: $3.00)

POTPOURRI. BLENDED AND ESSENTIAL OILS
SUPPLIES

Bonny Doon Farm
600 Marin Road
Santa Cruz, CA 95060
(Catalog available)

Hanna s Potpourri
Specialties Inc.
P.O. Box 3647
Fayetteville, AK 72702
(800) 327 9826

Herb Garden Fragrances
3744 Section Road
Cincinnati, OH 45236

Kiehl s
109 Third Avenue
New York, NY 10003

Lorann Oils
4518 Aurelius Road
P.O. Box 22009
Lansing, MI 48909-2009
(800) 248 1302

Mrs. O Quinn s Scent Shoppe
1908 Joanne Street
Wichita, KS 67203

Picture Acknowledgements
All photographs in this book were taken by John Freeman and Michelle Garrett, apart from those on pages 36 (left) and 37, 54 and 55 and pages 36 (right), 75
(hollyhocks), 77 (sea thrift), 81 (knapweed), 82 (chamomile), 87 (rocket), 90 (herb robert), 93 (woad), 95 (lavender), 98 (mallow), 107 (greater plantain), 113 (savory)
and 117 (variegated Russian comfrey) which were kindly lent by Jenny Balfour-Paul, Jacqui Hurst and the Garden Picture Library respectively. The pictures on pages 7
(bottom), 8 (top and bottom left) and 9 (right) were lent by Visual Arts Library.